Easy Does It® fo
Intermediate

by Barbara A. Roseman and Karin L. Johnson

Skill	Ages	Grades
■ fluency	■ 6 through 12	■ 1 through 7

Evidence-Based Practice

- ASHA (1995) promotes use of a hierarchy going from single words to conversation fluently, role-playing social situations to desensitize a patient's reaction to stuttering, and implementing parent and teacher support for carryover of targeted fluency skills.

- Stuttering therapy may focus on fluency-shaping techniques or stuttering modification techniques. Both techniques are evidence-based and involve key components of modeling and self-management or self-monitoring (Prins & Ingham, 2009).

- Laiho and Klippi (2007) found improvement in both the frequency and duration of stuttering moments in school-aged children involved in an intensive stuttering therapy program targeting stuttering modification.

- The speech-language pathologist must counsel the parents and the child who stutters with strategies to combat internal negative feelings, along with external negative reactions from others, including teasing. The child who stutters must feel free to express these emotions, otherwise he may continue to harbor internal negative feelings toward his stuttering which may prohibit him from progressing in fluency therapy (Ramig & Bennett, 1993).

- Use of fluent conversational skills, in various social situations relevant to the child, need to be directly addressed in therapy for successful transfer of targeted skills and discharge from speech therapy services (Weiss, 2004).

Easy Does It for Fluency Intermediate incorporates these principles and is also based on expert professional practice.

References

American Speech-Language-Hearing Association (ASHA). (1995). *Guidelines for practice in stuttering treatment*. Retrieved January 28, 2010, from www.asha.org/docs/pdf/GL1995-00048.pdf

Laiho, A., & Klippi, A. (2007). Long- and short-term results of children's and adolescents' therapy courses for stuttering. *International Journal of Language & Communication Disorders, 43*(3), 367-382.

Prins, D., & Ingham, R.J. (2009). Evidence-based treatment and stuttering-Historical perspective. *Journal of Speech, Language, and Hearing Research, 52*, 254-263.

Ramig, P.R., & Bennett, E.M. (1993). Working with 7-12-year-old children who stutter: Ideas for intervention in the public schools. *Language, Speech, and Hearing Services in the Schools, 26*, 138-150.

Weiss, A.L. (2004). Why we should consider pragmatics when planning treatment for children who stutter. *Language, Speech, and Hearing Services in Schools, 35*, 34-45.

LinguiSystems, Inc.
3100 4th Avenue
East Moline, IL 61244
800-776-4332

FAX: 800-577-4555
Email: service@linguisystems.com
Web: linguisystems.com

Printed in the U.S.A.

ISBN 10: 0-7606-0172-0
ISBN 13: 978-0-7606-0172-3

About the Authors

Barbara A. Roseman, M.A., CCC-SLP, is an associate professor at Augustana College in Rock Island, IL. She is also the director of the Augustana College Center for Communicative Disorders. Barbara is the past-president and Fellow of the Illinois Speech and Hearing Association.

Karin L. Johnson, M.A., CCC-SLP, is an associate professor at Augustana College in Rock Island, IL. She is also the director of the speech-language pathology program, the chair of the Department of Speech Communications and Theater Arts, and the chair of the Fine Arts Division at Augustana College.

Barbara and Karin have co-authored numerous publications in the areas of fluency disorders, motor speech disorders, narratives, birth-to-three intervention, and metalinguistics. These long-time LinguiSystems' authors have also written *The Fluency Companion* and *Easy Does It for Fluency—Preschool/Primary*.

Dedication
We dedicate this book to our parents: Edna R. Allen and the late Milton A. Allen, and Blenda L. and H. Milton Lundahl for their faith in us.

Acknowledgment
Appreciation to Laura, Sarah, Kathy, Cindy, and Bob for their enthusiastic support and encouragement.

Table of Contents

Introduction

Easy Does It for Fluency—Intermediate is an integrated approach to fluency therapy that will enable you to develop an individualized, systematic therapy program for students with stuttering disorders, ages 6 - 11. This program provides guidelines for organizing therapy, but it is not meant to be a "cookbook." As written, it will allow you flexibility when planning therapy so you can tailor it to fit each student's needs. (Materials are provided, but feel free to supplement with similar activities of your choosing.) An attempt has been made to anticipate problems which might arise, and to offer suggestions for how to deal with them. We have also included suggestions for ways to gain support from family members and school personnel.

Rationale

Easy Does It for Fluency—Intermediate integrates concepts from fluency shaping and stuttering modification. It is based on the premise that all therapy techniques modify a student's speech production in one way or another. *Easy Does It for Fluency—Intermediate* will enable you to focus on forward flowing speech or word-initiation techniques or both, depending on the needs of each student.

This program addresses three components usually theorized as potential causes of stuttering:

- motor
- linguistic
- psychosocial

The motor component focuses on rate control and continuous phonation. In addition, a relaxed approach to word initiation is used in the techniques of bouncing, sliding, easy onsets, and light contacts.

The linguistic component includes activities that are designed in hierarchies that control for length and complexity of responses. The activities have been selected to emphasize language skills related to vocabulary; associations; verbal problem solving; and conversational, narrative, and expository discourse related to the pragmatic functions of informing, controlling, expressing feelings, ritualizing, and imagining.

The psychosocial component works on developing positive attitudes and reducing emotional reactions. Activities are designed to desensitize the student to potential fluency disrupters. Throughout the program, the student is encouraged to take responsibility for the changes to be made, and to become his own advocate.

Easy Does It for Fluency—Intermediate is a direct approach to therapy. A student in the 6-11 age range is usually aware of the stuttering and is able to confront it directly. A student needs to identify what he does when stuttering and determine what needs to be changed. The student needs to take an active role in all parts of the therapy program. Such a student is still in the concrete operation stage of development (Piaget: *The Language and Thought of the Child*[1]), therefore, the approaches used in this program provide the student with concrete approaches to attitudes and techniques. The student is encouraged throughout to verbalize goals and target behaviors as well as self-instruct, self-monitor, and self-reinforce.

[1]Piaget, Jean). *The Language and Thought of the Child.* Cleveland, OH: The World Publishing Company 1955.

Basic Principles

Easy Does It for Fluency—Intermediate uses modeling as its basic principle. Throughout the program, you need to model techniques, attitudes, and behaviors conducive to fluency development. Since a student at this stage is old enough and aware enough to confront stuttering directly, verbal and concrete reinforcement may be used to enhance learning. While concrete reinforcement is usually not necessary, it has been found to be helpful with some students during the establishment step.

Step 1: Getting Ready
The student is prepared for the therapeutic process.

Step 2: Analyzing
The student learns to distinguish between fluent speech with easy disfluencies and stuttering. Terminology used throughout the program is learned.

Step 3: Modifying Speech Production
The student learns to modify speech production by using forward flowing speaking, word-initiation techniques, or both in structured activities.

Step 4: Desensitizing
The student learns to use modified speech patterns in the presence of fluency disrupters.

Step 5: Transferring
The student learns to use modified speech patterns in real-life situations in the home, school, and community.

Step 6: Maintaining
The student is encouraged to use the new speaking patterns while gradually decreasing the need for direct therapy.

Easy Does It for Fluency—Intermediate progresses in order from Step 1 through Step 6 with some overlap. For example, work on transferring begins subtly in Step 3, Modifying. Work on desensitizing (Step 4) continues in Step 5, but within the more natural framework of the activities rather than in the contrived manner used in Step 4.

No time frames have been provided as each student will progress at an individual pace. Early steps will be completed more quickly than later steps. Alert the student to this fact when you begin the program.

When beginning this program, daily therapy is ideal. If daily therapy is not possible, therapy should be scheduled for at least two half-hour sessions per week. Individual sessions should be scheduled for Steps 1-4 (Objective 1) if at all possible. Once the student has achieved success with a peer or small group, group sessions might be valuable once a week. Some individual therapy should continue at least once a week throughout the entire program. Many activities late in the program can be adapted for full class collaborative sessions.

6

Assessing Progress

It's important to remember that this is a flexible program; therefore, criteria for completion of each step are not provided. Work should be presented in such a way that the student achieves a high degree of fluency in each task. If the student has difficulty, adjust work to an easier level to assure success. If the student easily completes an activity, introduce a slightly more complex task. Periodic fluency sampling of spontaneous speech and graphing of the percentage of disfluent behaviors have been found to be effective methods of judging progress.

In general, a student is ready for dismissal when:
1. spontaneous speech has fewer than two part-word repetitions per 100 words, fewer than one prolongation per 100 words, and no struggle behaviors
2. the student demonstrates use of and tolerance for easy disfluencies
3. you, the student, and outside support providers feel that the student's speech is within a normal range for his age, or is sufficiently fluent that the student feels comfortable speaking in any situation

Attitudes/Advocacy

Easy Does It for Fluency—Intermediate recognizes the need for developing positive attitudes not only in the student but also in the family and school. In addition, it recognizes the need for students to become their own advocates and for family members and school support persons to advocate for them, too. The Home and School Letters, pages 146 - 165, will guide the family and school personnel in developing positive attitudes regarding stuttering and in taking a proactive approach to situations in which the student who stutters is involved. To set the tone, share Home Letter A and School Letter A, pages 146 - 147, at the outset of the therapy program.

Similarly throughout the program, educate the student about the process of therapy and encourage him to participate in all aspects of the process. By teaching the student about stuttering, many of the negative feelings toward stuttering will be eliminated. By giving the student an active role in the therapeutic process, the student will gain a sense of self-control.

Support Providers

Easy Does It for Fluency—Intermediate recognizes the need for outside support for students who are working on fluency development. Clinical experience has shown that students who have interested adults at home and at school make the most progress. Suggestions for educating home and school support providers about the nature of the therapy, securing their input and participation, and encouraging them in their roles as reinforcers are included.

Have the student identify potential home and school support providers. Schedule conferences with these people to explain the need for their involvement. Ask for regular input and feedback.

We hope you find this program as helpful in planning your therapy as we have. Use it as a guide to plan an individualized therapy program for each child. Feel free to add your own creative touches!

Barbara and Karin

7

Step 1: Getting Ready

> **Goal:** The student will be prepared for the therapeutic process.

During this step, the student will decide whether to make a commitment to learning to use easy speech. Before a decision is made, educate the student about the process of developing easy speech by defining terms, identifying goals and target behaviors, and having the student experience easy speech. Let the student know that the goal of developing easy speech doesn't involve achieving perfect fluency — no one has perfect fluency. Instead, while some speech will be fluent, easy disfluencies will also be present.

Often, this step is completed at the end of the evaluation or in the conference following the evaluation. This could also be done in conjunction with a parent conference. We have found, however, that it is wise to speak to the student and parent(s) separately and then talk with them jointly.

Suggestions for Support Providers

Send Home Letter 1 and School Letter 1, pages 148 - 149. These letters describe the therapy program. They also suggest that a family member and/or student's teacher(s) join the session to observe the use of easy speech in unison responses. If an observation isn't possible, meet in a convenient location to explain and model the use of easy speech.

Consider involving family members/significant others in family support and/or family counseling programs you have developed. Also, consider programs to inform school personnel about the identification and management of stuttering and possible collaboration activities. You might also develop a program to inform students about communication difference[1].

In addition, consider developing a questionnaire which could be sent to the family and/or school personnel. It asks them to list people with whom the student has contact, places the student is likely to frequent, and situations in which the student speaks or is expected to speak[1].
Suggest to the student's teacher(s) that unison or choral responses be used in the class whenever possible. Be sure that the teacher maintains confidentiality about why this is being done.

> **Objective 1:** The student will demonstrate understanding of the terminology associated with the therapy process.

Procedure

The student will learn the terminology associated with the therapy process. Give the student definitions for *fluency* and *disfluency*. Explain to him how to differentiate types of disfluency using definitions for easy disfluencies and stuttering disfluencies. Also, explain that the use of easy speech will be the goal of therapy should he decide to make a commitment. Finally, have the student demonstrate an understanding of the terms by matching definitions.

---

[1]These types of programs and a questionnaire found in *The Fluency Companion*, LinguiSystems 1994, may be used or you can develop your own.

Attitudes/Advocacy

Let the student know that there are a number of famous people who have been reported to have stuttered:

Aristotle	(Greek philosopher)
Clara Barton	(founded the Red Cross)
Winston Churchill	(former prime minister of England)
Louis Carroll	(author of *Alice in Wonderland*)
Charles Darwin	(British scientist)
James Earl Jones	(actor - voice of Darth Vader)
Bob Love	(former Chicago Bulls basketball player)
Marilyn Monroe	(actress)
Isaac Newton	(English scientist)
Carly Simon	(singer)

Talk to the student about attitudes. Cut out the following attitudes from Attitude Cards, Materials Book, page 8. Mount them on index cards and suggest they be placed where the student will see them often (e.g., notebook, bulletin board).

Stuttering is something I do. I can change how I talk.
I can learn to talk in an easy way.
I can't stutter and talk easily at the same time. I will choose to talk easily.
I can learn easy speech one step at a time.
I can decide how I'll talk.

Finally, reassure the student that there's nothing wrong with him; he isn't dumb, bad, or physically impaired because he stutters sometimes. Instead, reassure him that he is good, bright, and healthy. He just needs to learn a new habit and you'd like to help.

Activity

Materials: Definitions, Materials Book, page 9; chalkboard or blank sheet of paper

Homework: none

Directions: Begin by explaining to the student what he will learn in speech class. Demonstrate each of the terms on the activity sheet. Show the activity sheet to the student.

Fluency means the flow of speech, the way one word flows into the next word and one sentence flows into the next sentence.

Disfluency means that there's a break in the flow of speech. Some disfluencies are okay to have in our speech. They're called *easy disfluencies*. Everyone has them sometimes. They're part of easy talking.

Stuttering means disfluencies in the flow of speech that are not easy and which most people don't have.

Easy speech is our goal in therapy. Easy speech is speech with easy disfluencies.

Write the words *fluency, disfluency, easy disfluency,* and *stuttering disfluency* across the top of the chalkboard or the sheet of paper. Have the student write each of the following phrases under the word it describes.

easy flow of speech	(fluency)
break in flow of speech	(disfluency)
okay to have in your speech	(easy disfluency)
Everyone has this sometimes.	(easy disfluency)
easy break in flow of speech	(easy disfluency)
a hard or tense break in the flow of speech	(stuttering disfluency)
Most people don't do this.	(stuttering disfluency)

Now, write the word *Goal* at the bottom of the paper. Ask the student what the goal of therapy will be. Then, have the student define the goal as easy speech or speech with easy disfluencies.

Objective 2: The student will experience fluency.

Procedure

Have the student join you in some unison responses as you model easy speech. After he has completed each activity, talk to him about the fluency he has achieved and why he was successful. Reassure the student that just because he stutters sometimes, there's nothing wrong with him. Explain that he just needs to learn a new habit and you'd like to help.

What if the student doesn't appear to need to do all of the unison responses? That's fine. Do only as many of the response tasks as necessary to show the student that he can be fluent and that he can achieve increased fluency by using an easy way of talking.

What if the student is using a soft voice when doing unison responses? That's fine, but be sure that you model a "typical" loudness level which is easy (tension free) and slow (90 - 110 words per minute or 120 - 140 syllables per minute). Be sure the student is talking, and not whispering.

Activity

Materials: none

Homework: none

Directions: Explain to the student that you're going to do some easy talking together. Do as many of the following activities as needed in unison with the student.

10

- counting
- singing of familiar songs
- reciting of familiar passages

After each activity, emphasize to the student that he was fluent, he used easy speech, and he made the words flow forward, one into the next.

> **Objective 3:** The student will understand the steps involved in the therapeutic process.

Procedure

Help the student learn the steps needed to achieve the goal of easy speech. Explain to the student that it will take time to reach the goal. Reassure the student that you'll help him achieve his goal, but he'll be doing the work.

Activity

Materials: Steps to Easy Speech, Materials Book, page 10

Homework: none

Directions: Explain to the student that he can learn to use easy speech instead of stuttering by working step-by-step to achieve his goal. Remind the student that it will take time just like learning any new habit takes time. Talk about how learning to use easy speech is like learning to play basketball, play the piano, or write in cursive.

Then, show the student the activity sheet. Talk about each of the steps. You might say, "We'll learn exactly what is involved if we use easy speech when we talk or if we stutter when we talk. Then, we'll practice easy speech in some activities. After you can do easy speech, we'll practice using it while I add some disrupters that might make you forget. Disrupters include people, noise, and interruptions. Finally, we'll practice using easy speech in real-life situations."

Emphasize that it will take time to learn how to use easy speech and time to remember to use it when speaking. Progress will be made one step at a time. Review the activity sheet. Tell the student that you'll show him how he's doing. As each step has been achieved, it will be checked off.

Finally, ask the student to tell you which sentences in the first step describe what he has already learned. Wait for a response. Then, remind the student that you can help him learn to use easy speech just like a coach or teacher helps him to learn other things, but that he will do the work.

11

Objective 4: The student will demonstrate a commitment to the therapeutic process.

Procedure

Talk to the student about signing a contract if he chooses to participate in therapy.

What if the student decides not to enroll? Accept the decision. Discuss it with the student and then check with him in a few months to see if he has changed his mind. Be sure to let the student know that you like him, even if he chooses not to enroll in therapy and even if he stutters. Encourage the student not to force his speech while he's talking. Let the student know that if he stutters, it's okay, but that he should attempt to stutter in an easy way.

Activity

Materials: Speech Contract, Materials Book, page 11

Homework: none

Directions: Tell the student again that you would like to help him learn easy speech. Ask the student if he'd like to learn how to use it. Give the student specific information about your plan for therapy such as how often you would work together. Be sure to let him know that others close to him will also be involved in the therapy process and that you'll be maintaining contact with them. Tell the student that specific times for therapy will be worked out if he decides to enroll. Be sure to obtain input from the student as well as the parent(s) and teachers involved. Encourage the student to ask questions.

Show the student the contract and explain it. Ask the student if he'd like to begin therapy. If so, ask him to sign it. Immediately begin setting up therapy.

If the student isn't ready to make a commitment, suggest that he think about it for awhile. Suggest that he talk to people who are important to him. Finally, tell the student that you'll check back in a few days to see if he has made a decision.

Step 2: Analyzing

> **Goal:** The student will distinguish easy speech from stuttering.

During this step, review the definitions of and model *easy disfluencies* and *stuttering disfluencies* for the student. Guide the student through activities which involve the identification of easy and stuttering disfluencies in your speech and in her own speech. Be sure to stress attitudes.

Suggestions for Support Providers

Send Home Letter 2 and School Letter 2, pages 150 - 151. Invite a parent to attend a session. After reviewing the terminology, ask the student to identify types of disfluencies as you demonstrate them.

Consider conducting an in-service for school personnel involved with the student to address identification and management of stuttering[1].

> **Objective 1:** The student will identify easy disfluencies and stuttering disfluencies in the clinician's speech.

Procedure

Review the definitions of *fluency, disfluency/easy disfluency,* and *stuttering disfluency*. The student will listen as you demonstrate easy disfluencies and stuttering disfluencies. Work with the student to label each disfluency. Then, identify struggle behaviors. Ask the student if she recognizes any stuttering disfluencies or struggle behaviors in her speech.

What if the student can't remember the "technical" names? Use descriptions. Encourage the student to describe what she does or hears. Then, provide the label.

What if the student says she doesn't stutter or reports using only some of the characteristics she actually uses in her speech when she listens to you or the audiotape of your speech? At this point, accept the student's analysis. Later, in Objective 2, if she misses characteristics when attempting to identify them on her own tape, identify them for her.

Attitudes/Advocacy

Write the statements, listed on the next page, on index cards. (They are found in larger type in the Materials Book, page 12, if you prefer to copy, cut apart, and mount them on index cards.) Talk about them with the student. Ask the student to place them in a location where she'll see them often (e.g., bathroom mirror, notebook, bulletin board, refrigerator).

---

[1] In-service information found in *The Fluency Companion*, also published by LinguiSystems 1994, may be used or you can create your own.

- I can describe easy speech.
- Everyone is disfluent at times.
- I can describe easy disfluencies and stuttering disfluencies.

Activity 1

Materials: Definitions, Materials Book, page 9

Homework: none

Directions: Use the activity sheet to review the definitions of *fluency*, *disfluency/easy disfluency*, and *stuttering disfluency*.

1. *Fluency:* You might say, "Let's review the words we learned last time. *Fluency* is the first word. It means the flow of speech, the way one word flows into the next word and one sentence flows into the next sentence. No one has perfect fluency."

2. *Disfluency:* "The second word is *disfluency*. A disfluency is a break in the flow of speech. Some disfluencies are okay to have in your speech. They are called *easy disfluencies*. Everybody has them sometimes. Let's talk about easy disfluencies." Write examples of easy disfluencies on the activity sheet under the definition or ask the student to do so.

"As we talk about easy disfluencies, I'll give you an example of each of them.

"It's okay to start talking, stop, and then start over again. This is called a *revision*. An example of a revision is: 'I walked — no I ran to the store. My brother — no, I mean my sister ran with me.'

"Sometimes we add extra sounds or words while we're talking. This is called an *interjection*. An example of an interjection is: 'I wanted some popcorn — um — to eat at the movie, but I — well — I didn't — you know — have any money.'

"It's also okay to say a word two or three times if you say it easily and rhythmically. This is called a *whole-word repetition*. An example of a whole-word repetition is: 'I-I-I did know your name, but, but I forgot it.'

"Often we repeat two or three words at a time. This is called *phrase repetition*. An example of phrase repetition is: 'And then, and then, and then she hit the ball really far!'

"*Hesitations* are also okay. These are short, relaxed pauses between words. An example of a hesitation is: 'I told (pause) my teacher that I forgot (pause) my homework.'

Do you have any of these disfluencies in your speech? Sure you do. So do I. Everybody does."

NOTE: If you think you might be introducing word-initiation modifications later, share the following information at this time. If you choose not to do so now, refer back to this information when you address it later in therapy.

Word-initiation Modifications

Explain to the student that there are also four other kinds of easy talking some people do. You might say the following:

"It's okay to repeat the beginning part of a word if it's repeated only once or twice and it's easy repeating. We call it *bouncing*. An example of bouncing is: 'We ca-ca-can't find the ball.'

"It's okay to hold out a sound if it's short and easy. It's like sliding into a word. We call it *sliding*. An example of sliding is: 'My name's S—-andra.'

"There are two other techniques which you can use to say any word. One of them involves bringing your vocal folds together easily. We call this *easy onset* and we use it on words that begin with vowels." Demonstrate and contrast easy onsets with hard attacks.

"The second technique which can be used to say any word involves bringing our speech helpers together easily. Speech helpers include our lips and our tongue. We call this *light contact* and we use it on words that begin with consonants." Demonstrate and contrast hard contacts and light contacts.

3. *Stuttering*: "There are also disfluencies that are not easy. They're tense and longer than easy disfluencies. Most people don't have them in their speech. These are called *hard* or *stuttering disfluencies*. Sometimes we just say *stuttering*." Write or have the student write the following stuttering disfluency types under the definition.

"If a word is said over and over and over again (more than three times), it's a *multiple whole-word repetition*. Usually, it's tense with an irregular rhythm. An example of a multiple whole-word repetition is: 'I-I-I-I-I-I don't want to.'

"If part of a word, a sound, or a syllable is said over and over again, it's a *part-word repetition*. It, too, is usually tense with an irregular rhythm. An example of a part-word repetition is: 'li-li-li-li-like.'

"Sometimes a sound is held too long a time. Usually, a person pushes too hard when making the sound. This is called a *prolongation*. An example of a prolongation is: 'N-------o, it's m-----ine.'

"At other times, an attempt is made to push speech out but nothing happens. It's different from a pause or hesitation because the person is tense when trying to talk. This is called a *silent block*. An example of a silent block is: 'I (silent block) can't find him.' If you make a hard attack on a vowel or a hard attack on a consonant and you get stuck, it's a silent block."

Now, go through each of the definitions again with the student. Ask the student to identify any easy disfluencies she has had. Then, have her identify any stuttering disfluencies she has had. Have the student put a check mark beside each type identified.

Activity 2

Materials: Analysis of Disfluencies and Identification Practice, Materials Book, pages 13 - 14; tape recorder.

Homework: none

Directions: Give the student the Analysis of Disfluencies activity sheet. Ask the student to listen to you as you say some sentences. Tape record it so you can listen to it again.

Read the sentences below and have the student decide if there is an easy disfluency or a stuttering disfluency in the sentence. Then, have the student label the type of easy disfluency or stuttering disfluency.

Sentence	Disfluency	Type
1. Miguel and-and-and Dad looked at the clubhouse.	easy	whole-word repetition
2. "I think I should pa-pa-pa-pa-paint it," said Miguel.	hard	part-word repetition
3. "Do you, do you have any leftover paint, Dad?"	easy	phrase repetition
4. "You can have this blue paint," s-------said Dad.	hard	prolongation
5. "Don't forget to, uh, stir it."	easy	interjection
6. "Good idea," said Dad, I mean, Miguel.	easy	revision
7. Miguel found a paintbrush (pause) and a stick.	easy	hesitation
8. He brought it to-to-to-to the clubhouse.	hard	multiple whole-word repetition
9. Miguel painted for (silent block) about two hours.	hard	silent block
10. Then, he ate lu-lunch.	easy	bouncing
11. (easy onset) After another hour, Miguel finished painting.	easy	easy onset
12. "Da-da-da-da-Dad," he called.	hard	part-word repetition
13. "Come (slide) s—-see the clubhouse."	easy	slide
14. "It looks (silent block) great," said Dad.	hard	silent block
15. "You should be (light contact) proud!"	easy	light contact

Continue to provide examples until you're sure that the student can recognize easy disfluencies and stuttering.

Finally, if your child has secondary characteristics, talk about other things people might do when they stutter. Show the student the line on the hard talking side of the Analysis of Disfluencies activity sheet. Tell the student that everything above it concerns stuttering behaviors connected to the sounds or words you make when you talk. Below the line are stuttering behaviors which occur when people push too hard and begin to do things with their bodies.

You might say, "Stuttering is connected to the sounds or words we say when we talk. But sometimes people use parts of their body when they stutter. This usually happens when they push really hard to talk. For example, someone might have difficulty saying the words and also (demonstrate as many as you think will be beneficial):

- move her arms or legs
- take a deep breath
- move her head
- close her eyes
- push with her lips

"These behaviors can become part of stuttering. Do you do any of these things when you stutter? Do you do anything else?

"In this class, we're going to learn to use easy speech. We'll concentrate on talking in an easy way. Our goal is to use easy disfluencies when we talk, not stuttering disfluencies."

Objective 2: The student will identify easy disfluencies and stuttering disfluencies in her own speech.

Procedure

The student will identify and differentiate easy disfluencies from stuttering disfluencies in her own speech by analyzing a tape recording made when she was talking and/or reading. Then, the student will analyze each disfluency by type.

What if the student resists analyzing her own speech? Analyze your speech again matter-of-factly. Then, try analyzing her speech again. If the student continues to resist, but has successfully analyzed your speech, skip this objective and go on to Objective 3.

Activity

Materials: Analysis of Disfluencies, Materials Book, page 13; tape recorder

Homework: none

Directions: Tape record the student while he's talking with you or reading. Give the student the activity sheet on which you listed the disfluencies found in your speech and play back the tape. Ask the student to stop the tape whenever she hears disfluencies and determine whether she hears easy disfluencies or stuttering disfluencies. Then, ask the student to identify the types of disfluencies heard on the tape.

You might say, "I want you to read (talk) to me. I'm going to record you." Make the tape. "Now, I want you to play the tape back. Anytime you hear a disfluency, stop the tape." When the student stops the tape, you might say, "Good. Yes, that was a disfluency. Was it an easy disfluency or a stuttering disfluency?" Wait. Then say, "Let's put a check mark by the type of (easy or stuttering) disfluency you heard." If the student doesn't identify the disfluency, help her describe what she heard and then help her find the correct type.

Objective 3: The student will identify easy disfluencies and stuttering disfluencies in the speech of others.

Procedure

Have the student listen to speakers outside of the therapy session to practice listening to disfluencies. The student will list types on an activity sheet.

17

Activity 1

Materials: Observation Analysis, Materials Book, page 15

Homework: Observation Analysis, Materials Book, page 15

Directions: Remind the student that everybody has disfluencies. Tell her to choose two or three television shows to watch. While listening/watching, have her determine if she hears any disfluencies. Be sure that the student is aware that most disfluencies heard will be easy disfluencies because stuttering disfluencies are not that common.

Each time the student hears a disfluency, tell her to determine if it's an easy disfluency or a stuttering disfluency. Tell her to record the type of disfluency on the activity sheet.

Note: You might want to go over the list of famous people who have been reported to have had stuttering disfluencies before the student leaves to reassure her that she isn't the only person who has stuttering disfluencies.

Activity 2

Materials: Identification Practice, Materials Book, page 14

Homework: Identification Practice, Materials Book, page 14

Directions: Review the differences between easy disfluencies and hard or stuttering disfluencies. Then, show the activity sheet to the student.

Explain to the student that you would like her to take the activity sheet home and write *hard* underneath the pictures of the people using hard disfluencies and *easy* under the people using easy disfluencies. Have the student review the activity sheet with a parent/significant other before bringing it to the next session.

Step 3: Modifying Speech Production

> **Goal:** The student will produce easy speech by modifying speech production through:
>
> 1) a forward flowing speech technique,
> 2) word-initiation techniques of bouncing, sliding, light contacts, and easy onsets, or
> 3) both

This goal may be approached through three different paths. If the student has a mild to moderate severity rating and little emotional reactions, you may want to focus first (and maybe only) on Path 1 which uses a forward flowing speech technique.

If the student has a moderate to severe rating and/or significant emotional reactions, you may want to focus first (and maybe only) on Path 2 which uses word-initiation techniques.

If you begin Path 1 or Path 2 and feel the need to supplement your work with the other approach to modification, Path 3 provides suggestions for how to do this.

Regardless of the path you choose, it's important to approach the work as a means of modifying speech production. In this way, you can easily move back and forth without conveying the idea to the student that he has failed with one technique and has to try something else. Instead, simply offer another type of modification to provide the student with additional alternatives for achieving control.

Path 1

> **Goal 3.1:** The student will produce easy speech in structured activities by modifying speech production through the use of forward flowing speech.

In this part of step 3, model forward flowing speech for the student. Forward flowing speech is slow, easy speech. Initially, it's produced at a rate of 90 - 110 words per minute. (To get a sense for this rate, select a passage with 100 words in it. Using a stopwatch, read the passage. If it takes you less than a minute, you are speaking too rapidly.) As the student progresses through the steps, the rate may increase to a rate that seems comfortable for the student (a rate at which he is able to maintain fluency). You should, however, continue to model a rate slower than the student's habitual rate. Continuous phonation (running all the words together) is stressed.

The motor component of speech is addressed by adjusting the rate and focusing on continuous phonation. The linguistic component is addressed by controlling the length and complexity of the tasks used to practice the target behaviors. The psychosocial component is addressed by using hierarchies and familiar materials. This enhances the student's chances for success and builds his confidence. You will also build his confidence by providing a clear model and positive feedback.

Finally, by enlisting the student's participation in self-instructing, self-reinforcing, and in planning practice, you'll be helping the student assume responsibility and become his own advocate.

Attitudes/Advocacy

Throughout this objective, stress to the student that he can control speech production by slowing his speaking rate and running his words together. Stress the importance of forward movement during speech production. Send home some of the positive attitudes found in the Materials Book, page 16. Suggest that the student put them in places where he can read them often (e.g., on the mirror or on a book).

Attitudes include:

- Good things come from practice.
- It's all right to lose. There is fun in playing, not just in winning.
- No one is perfect. Everyone makes mistakes. We can learn from our mistakes.
- Practice! Practice! Practice! Learning a new habit takes practice.

Continue to have the student self-instruct and self-evaluate. Remind the student of the need to practice many times in order to develop new habits of forward flowing speech to replace the old habits of hard speech. Be sure to have the student check off each objective on the Steps to Easy Speech chart, Materials Book, page 10, as a step is completed so he's aware of the progress being made.

If you know a student or adult who has learned to use forward flowing speech, invite the person to join the session and demonstrate the forward flowing speech for the student.

Suggestions for Support Providers

Share Home Letter 3.1-A and School Letter 3.1-A, pages 152 - 153, so parents, significant others, and the student's teacher(s) will know what the student will be focusing on when practicing forward flowing speech. Be sure the student shares Introducing Forward Flowing Speech (Materials Book, page 18) at home and at school. If you decide to introduce prolonged speech, also share Home Letter 3.1-B and School Letter 3.1-B, pages 154 - 155. Be sure the student shares Introducing Prolonged Speech (Materials Book, page 20) at home and at school.

Invite parents, significant others, and the student's teacher(s) to observe all or part of a therapy session so they will understand the target behaviors and so the student can demonstrate how to use forward flowing speech in imitation first, then in carrier/stereotyped responses, questions and answers, and finally in short formulative responses.

Send home activities from the Materials Book in which the student has achieved success in therapy sessions. Make sure you send detailed information on how to use the activities at home so parents and significant others will know what to do and what to expect. Make sure they understand not to move beyond the level of response being targeted at the time (e.g., don't move into questions and answers or conversation when the student is only as far as carrier/stereotyped responses).

Ask the teacher to share a copy of the student's books so you can incorporate classroom vocabulary and topics into your materials. Talk with the teacher about ways to incorporate the response types into classroom activities. For example, imitation can easily be incorporated into activities in which students are asked to repeat definitions, assignments, or class rules.

Similarly, when the student is able to use forward flowing speech in stereotyped/carrier sentences with you and the teacher in therapy, perhaps the class could play a game for finding objects in the room or naming states that begin with a certain letter. Each student would respond using a carrier/stereotyped sentence such as, "I know something (or a state) that starts with the letter A. It is apple (or Alaska)." Other activities might include carrier sentences which each student would use such as, "I see a ___, I hear a ___, I'm thinking of ___, " or "My favorite ___, is ___ ."

For questions and answers, the teacher could have the class role play introductions. Each student would say, "My name is ___ . What is your name?" A similar procedure could be used to state preferences. For example, a student could say, "My favorite ___ is ___ . What is your favorite ___?" (This could be adapted to classroom topics such as presidents, states, animals, etc.) At this point, classroom assignments using What's Your Favorite? and Ask Me Questions can also be made. (Materials Book, pages 118 - 119).

Objective 1: The student will be introduced to forward flowing speech.

Procedure

Explain to the student that he's going to learn a new way of talking called *forward flowing speech.* Demonstrate the new way of talking using a slightly slower than usual rate combined with continuous phonation. The rate should be between 90 - 110 words per minute. Later, increase this rate slightly, but to begin, the rate needs to be enough slower than the student's habitual rate so he realizes there is a difference and so he can concentrate on the feel of moving forward in speech production. After demonstrating the forward flowing speech, move directly into Objective 2. Use Activities 1 and 2 to introduce forward flowing speech.

What if the student has trouble initiating a word? Try using an easy onset, light contact, or slide (refer to Path 2, pages 41 - 44 for definitions and directions regarding these techniques) in your modeling, but do not name them as techniques. Just have the student try to imitate your productions. If the student continues to have difficulty, consider changing to Path 2 or 3.

What if the student has trouble on certain sounds? Initially, eliminate words beginning with these sounds. Later, after the student has gained success and confidence in easy talking, gradually re-insert some of these words. If the student continues to have difficulty, consider changing to Path 2 or 3.

What if the student is fluent during activities but stutters in conversation? Do not be concerned. Keep the student on task as much as possible to reduce spontaneous speech. Suggest that you save conversation until the end of the session.

What if the student seems frustrated with stuttering in conversation? Remind the student that a new way of talking takes time. Progress comes in steps. Look at the Steps to Easy Speech, Materials Book, page 10, and review the progress being made. Let the student know he shouldn't expect fluent speech all the time yet. Stress the positive gains being made.

What if the family/teachers express concern over continued difficulty in conversation? Remind them that you don't expect transfer to real-life situations until much later in the program. Review the Steps to Easy Speech chart, Materials Book, page 10, and show them how continuous progress is occurring, but not to expect transfer yet.

What if the student seems tense? Consider introducing Relaxation Exercises, Materials Book, page 17.

What if the student uses a monotone? Encourage the student to vary his inflection. Exaggerate inflection patterns in your model.

What if the student whispers or speaks too softly in a breathy manner? Remind the student to use a normal volume and to "talk like I do." Be sure to model normal speaking patterns yourself. If necessary, model different loudness patterns in your speech and have the student imitate them so the student realizes that forward flowing speech can be produced softly or loudly.

What if the student doesn't establish eye contact? Encourage the student to look at you before responding throughout the program.

What if the student wants to move ahead too quickly or to converse too much? Remind the student of the need to practice a great deal on easier responses first so new habits can be strengthened. Tell the student that you need to complete the structured activities first, but that you will save time for conversation at the end.

What if the student has trouble producing forward flowing speech? Introduce prolonged speech in which three different rates are used. Tell the student, "Sometimes it's hard to learn forward flowing speech right away. It might be easier if we start even slower. We will learn *prolonged speech*. We'll begin with a super slow rate. Then, we will learn a medium slow rate, and then, a slightly slow rate." Directions for use of prolonged speech are included at the end of Objective 1 under Detour, page 23.

Activity 1

Materials: Introducing Forward Flowing Speech, Materials Book, page 18

Homework: Introducing Forward Flowing Speech, Materials Book, page 18

Directions: Tell the student, "We're going to learn an easy way to talk. It's called *forward flowing speech*. I want you to talk slowly and to run your sounds and words together like I do. Listen while I read these words, phrases, and sentences." Wait. "Now, I'll say them twice. Listen the first time and then say them with me the second time." Model a rate of 90 - 110 words per minute. Use continuous phonation throughout.

Activity 2

Materials: Practicing Forward Flowing Speech, Materials Book, page 19

Homework: Practicing Forward Flowing Speech, Materials Book, page 19

Directions: Tell the student, "We're going to learn an easy way to talk. I want you to talk slowly and to run your sounds and words together like I do. Listen while I name and describe these pictures."

Wait. "Now, I'll say them again twice. Listen the first time and then say them with me the second time." Model a rate of 90 - 110 words per minute. Be sure to phonate continuously as you model forward flowing speech.

Detour

If the student has difficulty understanding forward flowing speech, introduce prolonged speech in which three different rates are used. Tell the student, "Sometimes it's hard to learn forward flowing speech right away. It might be easier if we start even slower. We will learn *prolonged speech*. We'll begin with a super slow rate. Then, we will learn a medium slow rate, and then a slightly slow rate." Once the student masters slightly slow speech, return to forward flowing speech and resume the program with Objective 2, page 27.

Note: If you have access to a delayed auditory feedback machine, you may use it to help establish prolonged speech, but it isn't necessary. If used, it's suggested that you use only three rates as described under Objective 1-A, Procedure, page 23.

What if the student doesn't use continuous phonation? Use printed lines to illustrate that the words and syllables must run together (e.g., Look‿at‿us.). Also, have the student feel his throat to feel the vibrations associated with phonation.

What if the student succeeds at the slower rates but has difficulty at the slightly slow rate? Spend more time at the medium slow rate. Try exaggerating inflection patterns. Concentrate on the continuous phonation and idea of "forward flow." Consider changing the approach to Path 3 to break up old patterns of production.

Objective 1-A: The student will be introduced to prolonged speech as an intermediate step in establishing forward flowing speech.

Procedure

Begin with a very slow rate so the student can concentrate on the feel of his speech. This rate is **only** to be practiced in therapy. The student may react negatively if he thinks you're going to expect this kind of talking in public, so it's important for the student to realize that this type of speech is not to be practiced outside of therapy. The rate should be about 30 - 45 words per minute. At this rate, you can only produce about two to three words per breath. Remember to phonate continuously during the production. You might describe this feature as "dragged-out speech" (DOS) or simply say, "Run your words together slowly."

It will usually only take one session to introduce super slow speech (Activities 3 - 6, pages 24 - 25). It isn't recommended that you send the Super Slow Speech activity sheets home unless the student really wants to show his family what he's been learning **and** if the family support person(s) has attended a session where you and the student demonstrated super slow speech and explained the rationale.

At the next session, introduce a moderately slow rate of 60 - 75 words per minute. This rate also should only be practiced in therapy. Begin this session by reviewing super slow speech and then introduce medium slow speech by using Activities 7 - 9, pages 25 - 26. This, too, will usually only take one day. As noted above, the associated activity sheets should not be sent home unless the student really wants to show the family support person(s) **and** only if the support person(s) has attended a session where you and the student demonstrated medium slow speech and explained the rationale.

During the following session, introduce slightly slow speech at a rate of 90 - 110 words per minute, which is the same as forward flowing speech. Begin this session by reviewing super slow speech and medium slow speech. Then, practice slightly slow speech using Activities 10 - 11, pages 26 - 27. Remind the student to speak slowly and to run the words together. Again, this will usually only take one day. Since slightly slow speech is a socially acceptable rate, activity sheets may be sent home if desired, but it isn't necessary.

In the fourth session, review the three rates. Then, spend some time alternating the very slow and slightly slow rates to be sure the student understands the need to control for rate and continuous phonation and to prevent him from slipping into old habits at the more normal rate. In this way, the student will gain confidence in his ability to control speech production. Use Activity 12, page 27, to practice alternating from super slow speech to slightly slow speech. Typically, you won't send the associated activity sheets home.

After the student can alternate between the two rates, tell the student that slightly slow speech is the same as forward flowing speech. Tell him that from now on you'll practice this rate. It's a socially acceptable rate and can be used anywhere.

Activity 3

Materials: Introducing Prolonged Speech, Materials Book, page 20

Homework: Introducing Prolonged Speech, Materials Book, page 20

Directions: Tell the student, "We're going to learn a new way to modify our speech called *prolonged speech*. We'll practice prolonged speech at three speeds. We'll start with super slow speech today. Next, we'll learn medium slow speech and last we'll learn slightly slow speech. I'll show you how to do each one and then we'll practice together. Listen."

Demonstrate each rate, being sure to speak slowly and to run your words together. Explain to the student, "Super slow speech and medium slow speech are too slow to use outside our room. We need to practice them, though, so we can concentrate on how our speech feels as we let our speech flow forward. When we start to use slightly slow speech, it will sound more normal. For today, though, we need to practice super slow speech." Move directly into Activity 4.

Activity 4

Materials: Practicing Super Slow Speech: Reading, Materials Book, page 21

Homework: none

Directions: Tell the student that you will use the activity sheet to practice reading in super slow speech. Remind the student to speak very slowly and to run his words together just like you do. Take a breath at each /. Say, "Now, we / will practice / super slow speech / in imitation. / I'll read / these sentences / and then you / repeat them / just like I do."

After you read the sentences in imitation, say, "Now, let's try / taking turns. / I'll read / the first sentence / in super / slow speech. / Then, you read / the next sentence / in super / slow speech."

Activity 5

Materials: Practicing Super Slow Speech: Describing, Materials Book, page 22

Homework: none

Directions: Tell the student that you will use the activity sheet to practice describing pictures in super slow speech. Remind the student to speak very slowly (only two to three words per breath) and to run his words together just like you do. Take a breath at each /. Say, "Now, we will / practice super / slow speech / in imitation / as we describe / these pictures. / I'll describe / the picture / and then you / repeat what / I said / in super / slow speech / just like / I did. / 'Girl eating.' / Your turn."

After you have repeated the sentences, say, "Now, let's try / taking turns. / I'll describe / the first picture / in super / slow speech. / Then, you describe / the second / picture in / a sentence / just like me. / Remember to / use super / slow speech."

Activity 6

Materials: Practicing Super Slow Speech: Talking, Materials Book, page 23

Homework: none

Directions: Tell the student that you will use the activity sheet to practice talking in super slow speech. Remind the student to speak very slowly (only two to three words per breath) and to run his words together just like you do. Take a breath at each /. Say, "Now, we will / practice super / slow speech / as we ask / and answer / simple questions. / We will use / this activity sheet / to help us / remember / what to ask / and answer. / I'll start. / 'Today, I / came to school.' / Now, you / tell me / one thing / you did today." Wait. (If the student has trouble, say, "Let's say it together.") "Now, let's do / the next one."

Activity 7

Materials: Practicing Medium Slow Speech: Reading, Materials Book, page 24

Homework: none

Directions: At the beginning of this session, review super slow speech for one to two minutes. Model medium slow speech (about 60 - 75 words per minute) as you tell the student, "Today, we're going / to practice medium / slow speech. / This speech is a / little faster than / super slow speech, / but still too slow / to use outside our room. / We are practicing it / so you can learn / new habits of talking. / We want to concentrate / on talking slowly / and running our words / together so we can / move forward smoothly / when we talk. / When we used super / slow speech we could only / say two to three words / on a breath. / Now we can say / four to five words / on a breath. / I'll read a sentence / in medium slow speech. / Listen and then read / the sentence after me. / 'Boy playing football.' You say that." If the student does well, repeat the activity sheet but take turns reading the sentences in medium slow speech.

Activity 8

Materials: Practicing Medium Slow Speech: Describing, Materials Book, page 25

Homework: none

Directions: Model medium slow speech as you tell the student, "Now, let's practice / medium slow speech while / we describe these pictures. / I'll go first. / I'll describe each / picture twice. / Listen the first time / and then repeat what / I said after me." If the student does well, repeat the activity sheet but take turns describing the pictures using medium slow speech.

Activity 9

Materials: Practicing Medium Slow Speech: Talking, Materials Book, page 26

Homework: none

Directions: Show the student the activity sheet. Model medium slow speech as you tell the student "Now, let's practice / medium slow speech while / we just talk. / I'll go first. / I'll say, / 'At recess I like / to play kickball.' / Now you tell me / one thing you like / to do at recess." If the student does well, try some more. Be sure to model the type of response first.

Activity 10

Materials: Practicing Slightly Slow Speech: Reading, Materials Book, page 27

Homework: Practicing Slightly Slow Speech: Reading, Materials Book, page 27

Directions: At the beginning of this session take a couple of minutes to review super slow speech and medium slow speech. Then, tell the student, "Today, we're going to practice slightly slow speech. This is slightly slower than you usually talk, but not so slow it sounds funny. You could use this kind of easy speech anywhere. I'll read each sentence twice. Listen while I read the first time. Then, read the sentence after me. Remember to go a little slow and to run your words together. We want our speech to flow forward smoothly." If the student has no trouble, repeat the activity sheet but take turns reading the sentences in slightly slow speech.

Activity 11

Materials: Practicing Slightly Slow Speech: Describing, Materials Book, page 28

Homework Practicing Slightly Slow Speech: Describing, Materials Book, page 28

Directions: Model slightly slow speech as you tell the student, "Now, let's practice slightly slow speech as we describe these pictures. I'll describe each picture twice. Listen the first time and then describe the picture after me. Remember to talk slowly and to run your words together just like I do. 'The woman is vacuuming the living room.' Your turn." If the student has no trouble, repeat the activity sheet but take turns describing the pictures.

Activity 12

Materials: Practicing Slightly Slow Speech: Talking, Materials Book, page 29

Homework: Practicing Slightly Slow Speech: Talking, Materials Book, page 29

Directions: Model slightly slow speech as you tell the student, "Let's practice slightly slow speech as we talk." Show the student the activity sheet. "I'll tell you, 'My favorite sport is baseball' and I'll use slightly slow speech. Then, it will be your turn."

Activity 13

Materials: Alternating Super Slow and Slightly Slow Speech, Materials Book, page 30

Homework: none

Directions: At the beginning of this session, review the three rates for prolonged speech for one to two minutes each. Then, tell the student that he needs to practice switching from super slow speech to slightly slow speech so he really feels in control of his speech. Say, "I'll read these sentences (or describe these pictures) twice. I'll use super slow speech on the starred sentences and I'll use slightly slow speech on the other sentences. Listen the first time, then say what I say just like I do."

If the student has no trouble, repeat the activity sheets and take turns. Then, let the student try the paragraph. When you finish say, "Guess what. Did you realize that slightly slow speech is the same as forward flowing speech? From now on we'll just practice this kind of easy speech."

Now, begin working on Objective 2 using forward flowing speech as your target behavior. Remind the student often that you're learning easy speech by using forward flowing speech which involves speaking slowly and easily so that speech moves forward smoothly.

> **Objective 2:** The student will produce easy speech by imitating forward flowing speech in words, phrases, and sentences in structured activities.

Procedure

Model forward flowing speech in words, phrases, and sentences and have the student imitate your model. Stress two behaviors: slow and forward flowing. Use a rate of between 90 - 110 words per minute and use continuous phonation. After awhile, the rate may increase slightly as you and the student find the rate that is right for him. However, it should always be slightly slower than the old habitual rate.

Initially, exaggerate inflection patterns slightly so that the student gains experience in doing many things with speech. This will also help the student break up old patterns of speech production.

Begin by having the student imitate your forward flowing speech in words. Progress to phrases, carrier sentences (e.g., "I see a ___, I have a ___, This is a ___, Here is a __.") and then descriptive sentences. Use printed and pictured materials so the student practices forward flowing speech in both reading and speaking modalities.

Most students will succeed at imitation so you can quickly move to Objectives 3 - 5, pages 29 - 41. When beginning a new activity, return to imitation as you introduce the new vocabulary to reduce interference from problems with word retrieval or lack of vocabulary knowledge.

Be sure to explain the purpose of each objective and the target behaviors clearly. Have the student verbalize the target behaviors by asking, "What are the two things we are learning?" (*to speak slowly and easily*). Also, have the student self-instruct by asking, "What are we going to practice?" (*forward flowing speech*). Finally, ask the student to self-evaluate often by asking, "How do you think you did?"

Activity 1

Materials: any set of Matching Pictures or Memory Cards, Materials Book, pages 31 - 42 or 43 - 46

Homework: any set of Matching Pictures or Memory Cards, Materials Book, pages 31 - 42 or 43 - 46

Directions: Say, "I'm going to name and describe these pictures using forward flowing speech. Say what I say after me, just like I did. Remember to do two things: talk slowly and easily. What should you do?"

Be sure to progress from words ("ball"), to phrases ("big cat"), to carrier sentences ("I see a fish"), to descriptive sentences ("The elephant has a long trunk"). When finished, ask the student to self-evaluate.

Activity 2

Materials: appropriate Reading Practice activity sheets (Level A - Level C), Materials Book, pages 47 - 55

Homework: appropriate Reading Practice activity sheet, Materials Book, pages 47 - 55

Directions: Select reading activity sheets at or below the student's grade level so the student doesn't have to struggle with content. Level A is the easiest and Level C is the most difficult.

Say, "Let's practice easy talking as we read this page. I'll say the word (or phrase or sentence) and you say it after me, just like I did. Remember to do two things: talk slowly and easily. What should you do?" Remind the student to pause or take a breath if sentences are long. You could add / lines to indicate good places to pause or breathe. When finished, ask the student to self-evaluate.

Activity 3

Materials: any Unemotional Situation, Sequence, or Rebus Story, Materials Book, pages 56 - 69

Homework: any Unemotional Situation, Sequence, or Rebus Story, Materials Book, pages 56 - 69

Directions: Say, "I'm going to read this story using forward flowing speech. I'll read one sentence at a time. Say the sentence after me using forward flowing speech. What two things will you concentrate on?" (*slow and forward flowing speech*). When finished, ask the student to self-evaluate.

Objective 3: The student will produce easy speech by using forward flowing speech in carrier and stereotyped sentences in structured activities.

Procedure

Introduce a variety of activities in which the student can practice forward flowing speech while saying stereotyped sentences ("I pick a card, I found a piece, I want a picture, It goes here, I put it right here," or "Your turn.") and carrier sentences ("I found a ___ , This is a ___ , I need a ___ ," or "I have a ___ .")

Some activities will have a game format. If at all possible, arrange the activity so the student will win. This will help build confidence. Learning to remain fluent while dealing with competition comes in the next step. To prepare the student for losing, model good sportsmanship by saying things such as, "Oh well, I had fun anyway. It's fun to play even if you don't win," or "Maybe I'll win another day."

When introducing a new activity with unfamiliar vocabulary, review the new words in imitation first. Tell the student, "Let's practice forward flowing speech in imitation before we begin this activity. What two things do we want to do when we talk?" (*speak slowly and easily*). Periodically ask the student, "Why are we doing these activities?" (*to learn/practice easy talking; to build new patterns of easy talking*). Stress that it takes a lot of practice to learn new habits. Be sure to have the student self-evaluate from time to time by asking, "How did you do?"

Activity 1

Materials: any set of Matching Pictures, Materials Book, pages 31 - 42

Homework: any set of Matching Pictures, Materials Book, pages 31 - 42

Directions: If you think any of the words may be difficult or unfamiliar, go through them first and have the student imitate you as you say the words individually or in carrier sentences using forward flowing speech.

Make two copies of two different boards. Cut apart the pictures from one copy of each board. Place the other boards in front of you and the student. Mix up the cut-apart pictures and place them in a stack between you. Be sure one of your pictures is on the bottom.

Model forward flowing speech as you introduce the game by saying, "Now, we're going to practice forward flowing speech in some games. We'll use simple sentences over and over so it will be easy for you to concentrate on your forward flowing speech. On each turn we'll say, 'I pick a card. I need/don't need it. Your turn.'"

Remember to speak slowly and easily. Periodically, ask the student to verbalize why you're playing the game (*to practice forward flowing speech*) and what you are to do (*speak slowly and easily*). Also, remember to make comments such as, "I had fun even if I didn't win," or "Maybe I'll win next time."

Activity 2

Materials: any set of Memory Cards, Materials Book, pages 43 - 46

Homework: any set of Memory Cards, Materials Book, pages 43 - 46 (Cut apart and send home with instructions on how to play.)

Directions: If you think any of the words may be difficult or unfamiliar, have the student imitate you as you say them individually or in carrier sentences.

Make two copies of the cards and cut the pictures apart. Place the pictures facedown between you and the student.

Play a memory game using the pictures. Model forward flowing speech as you say, "Now, we're going to practice forward flowing speech while playing a memory game. We'll use short simple sentences so you can concentrate on speaking slowly and easily. On each turn we'll say, 'I pick a card. It is a ___. I pick another card. It is a ___. They do/do not match.' If they match, you get another turn. If not, turn the pictures facedown again and say, 'Your turn.'"

Try to allow the student to win so you can make positive attitude statements regarding competition.

Activity 3

Materials: any commercial board game or any Track Board Game and Track Board Sentences, Materials Book, pages 70 - 79; game markers, spinner or die

Homework: any Track Board Game and matching Track Board Sentences, Materials Book, pages 70 - 79

Directions: If you think any of the words may be difficult or unfamiliar, have the student imitate you as you say them individually or in carrier sentences. Then, tell the student that you're going to practice forward flowing speech in simple sentences while playing a Track Board Game.

Cut apart the Track Board Sentences. Place the game board between you and the student. Place the sentences in a pile to the side. Before each turn, select a track board sentence and use forward flowing speech while saying, "I pick a sentence. It says, 'Here is a car.' Now, I spin the spinner (or roll the die). I got a 4. I can move 4 spaces. Your turn." If a player lands on a space with a message, have the player read the message in forward flowing speech.

Periodically, ask the student to verbalize why you are playing the game (*to practice forward flowing speech*) and what the target behaviors are (*slow and forward flowing speech*). As you play, be sure to reinforce the student by saying, "I like the way you're using forward flowing speech." Also, occasionally ask the student to comment on how he is doing.

If possible, arrange for the student to win so you can model positive competitive remarks.

Activity 4

Materials: any Opposite Association Pictures or Words, Materials Book, pages 80 - 85; pencil

Homework: any Opposite Association Pictures or Words, Materials Book, pages 80 - 85

Directions: Have the student imitate your forward flowing speech as you name the opposites. Then, model forward flowing speech as you tell the student, "Today we're going to practice forward flowing speech in simple sentences while we find opposites. Here's what we'll say, 'This is a ___. The opposite of ___ is ___. Here is a ___. They go together. I'll draw a line between them. Your turn.'" Ask the student to tell you what kind of talking he should be using.

Activity 5

Materials: any Bingo Function Board and Bingo Function Cards, Materials Book, pages 86 - 89, and 90.

Homework: any Bingo Function Board and Bingo Function Cards, Materials Book, pages 86 - 89, and 90

Directions: Cut apart the Function Cards and circles. Read the Bingo Function Cards in forward flowing speech and have the student imitate you. Then, give each player a Bingo Function Board. Place the cards in a pile in the middle and put the circles to the side.

Tell the student, "Today, we're going to play a game using simple sentences so you can concentrate on using forward flowing speech. The game is like Bingo®. The first person to get five circles in a row (down, across, diagonally) is the winner. I'll go first and show you how to play. 'I pick a card. It says "something to pour." That's "milk." I found it on my board. I put a circle on it. You should put a circle on the milk on your board, too. Now, it's your turn.'"

Periodically, ask the student to tell you why you're playing the game and what the target behaviors are. Reinforce the student by saying, "I like the way you used forward flowing speech. You talked slowly and easily just like I did."

Activity 6

Materials: any Hidden Picture and Hidden Picture Objects and Words, Materials Book, pages 91 - 98

Homework: any Hidden Picture and Hidden Picture Objects and Words, Materials Book, pages 91 - 98

Directions: If you think the words may be difficult or unfamiliar, have the student imitate you as you name them or use them in carrier sentences.

Cut out the companion words or pictures. Use pictures for younger students and words for older students.

Put the hidden picture on the table and the accompanying pictures/words in a pile. Tell the student, "Today we'll practice forward flowing speech while we hunt for hidden objects. I'll show you how we play. 'I pick a picture (word). It is ___. I'm looking for ___. I found it. Your turn.'"

Periodically, ask the student to explain the kind of talking he is practicing. Be sure to reinforce the student by saying, "I like the way you used your forward flowing speech on that turn."

Activity 7

Materials: any Word Puzzle, Materials Book, pages 99 - 102

Homework: any Word Puzzle, Materials Book, pages 99 - 102

Directions: If you think any of the words may be difficult or unfamiliar, have the student imitate you as you name them individually or in carrier sentences.

Cut out the companion words and pictures. Use pictures for younger students and words for older students. Put a word puzzle on the table. Place the words or pictures in a pile.

Use forward flowing speech as you tell the student, "Today we're going to practice forward flowing speech while we do a word puzzle. Concentrate on using forward flowing speech just like me as we work. We'll say, 'I pick a card. It is a (says) ___. I'm looking for ___. I found it. It goes down. Your turn.' Remember that the words can go up, down, across, backwards, or diagonally."

Activity 8

Materials: Message Guessing 1 and 2, Materials Book, pages 103 - 104

Homework: Message Guessing 1, Materials Book, page 103 (Have the student create an original message for you to guess at the next session.)

Directions: Cut apart the messages. Use a pencil, chips, or circles from the Bingo Function Boards, Materials Book, pages 86 - 89, to mark the letters chosen and the number of guesses. Place one message in front of the student and Message Guessing 2 nearby.

Model forward flowing speech as you introduce the activity. Tell the student, "Today, we'll practice forward flowing speech while trying to figure out this message. You'll guess letters and if they're in the message, I'll fill them in. Keep track of the letters you choose on this sheet because you only get fifteen guesses. You can guess the message any time you think you know it. On each turn say, 'I want the letter ___.' When you want to guess, say, 'I want to guess the message. It says, ___.' Before we start, tell me why we're playing this game."

> **Objective 4:** The student will produce easy speech by using forward flowing speech while asking and answering questions in structured activities.

Procedure

Model forward flowing speech during questions and answers within the framework of structured activities. Many of the activities are the same as in Objective 3, but with questions and answers added to the format. Some new activities are also added. If you feel the words may be difficult or unfamiliar, have the student imitate your production of the words individually or in carrier sentences before beginning the activity.

In some instances, it's necessary to reverse roles in order for the student to ask the questions. In other activities, the questions are inherent in the game/activity.

Remember, some activities have a game format. If at all possible, arrange the activities so the student wins as you want to build confidence in this step. Learning to remain fluent while dealing with competition comes in the next step. To prepare the student for losing, model good sportsmanship by saying things such as, "Oh well, I had fun anyway. It's fun to play even if you don't win," or "Maybe I'll win another day."

Activity 1

Materials: any two sets of Matching Pictures, Materials Book, pages 31 - 42

Homework: any two sets of Matching Pictures, Materials Book, pages 31 - 42

Directions: Make two copies of two different boards. Cut apart the pictures from one copy of each board.

Tell the student that today you're going to incorporate questions and answers into your practice for forward flowing speech. Follow directions for this activity from Objective 3, Activity 2 (pages 29 - 30), but change the directions as follows: "Today, we'll say, 'I pick a card. I found a ___. Do you need it?'" Wait for a response. If the answer is "No," continue. "Do I need it? Yes I do. Now, it's your turn."

Model forward flowing speech throughout your turn and remind the student to use forward flowing speech during his turn. Reinforce the student for easy talking and ask the student to self-evaluate ("Did you remember your forward flowing speech?"). Be sure to ask for self-evaluation when the student has succeeded so the approach is a positive one. Remember to set up the game so the student wins. Provide positive attitude statements like, "It's fun to play even if you don't win."

Activity 2

Materials: none

Homework: none (Tell the student to play "I'm Thinking of . . ." at home or with friends.)

Directions: Model forward flowing speech as you describe this activity. Tell the student, "Today, we're going to practice forward flowing speech during an 'I'm Thinking of . . .' game. Here's what we do. Think of something in the room, but don't tell me what it is. I'll ask you questions to see if I can guess it. If I can't guess it after 10 questions, tell me the answer. I'll use forward flowing speech when I ask my questions. My first question is, 'What is it made of?' After I figure out what you're thinking of, it'll be your turn to ask me questions about something I'm thinking of."

Activity 3

Materials: Who's Guilty? 1 or 2, Materials Book, pages 105 - 106

Homework: Who's Guilty? 1 or 2, Materials Book, pages 105 - 106

Directions: Tell the student that today you'll practice forward flowing speech while playing "Who's Guilty?" Show the student one of the activity sheets. Have the student choose a person/animal on the sheet without telling you who/what it is. The person/animal the student chooses is guilty of a crime and you have to guess which one it is.

Ask questions using forward flowing speech to try to figure out who the guilty party is. The questions have to be answered with *yes* or *no*. You might want to use a pencil to cross out the pictures you eliminate.

Ask the student to tell you why you're playing this game (*to practice asking questions in forward flowing speech*) and what you are to concentrate on (*talking slowly and using forward moving speech*).

If the student has trouble asking questions that reduce the number of possibilities (e.g., questions specific to a picture such as "Is it the rhino?"), model questions related to categories (e.g., "Is it a boy?, Does the animal have two legs?", etc.).

Activity 4

Materials: any 20 Matching Pictures, Materials Book, pages 31 - 42

Homework: any 20 Matching Pictures, Materials Book, pages 31 - 42

Directions: Cut apart the pictures and place them on the table face up. Tell the student, "Today, we're going to play Ten Questions. We'll practice using forward flowing speech while we play. What do we do when we use forward flowing speech?" Wait for the answer.

"In this game, I'll think of one of these pictures. You have to ask questions to get clues to figure out which picture I'm thinking of. You can ask 10 questions and then you have to guess. You can guess sooner if you think you know which picture I'm thinking of. You can only ask questions that I can answer with *yes* or *no*. Don't forget to practice forward flowing speech when you ask the questions. I'll show you how. Think of a picture and I'll ask the questions. Then, it will be your turn."

If you select pictures within only one or two categories, most questions will relate to descriptions. If you mix pictures from several categories, you can also model questions related to categories and functions.

Activity 5

Materials: Riddles 1, 2, or 3, Materials Book, pages 107 - 109

Homework: Riddles 1, 2, or 3, Materials Book, pages 107 - 109

Directions: Cut apart the riddles. Use forward flowing speech as you tell the student, "Today we're going to practice forward flowing speech in questions while we ask each other riddles. Here is a pile of riddles. I'll take the first one and read the riddle. See if you can answer it. Use forward flowing speech in your answer." After your turn, say, "Now you pick a riddle and read it to me using forward flowing speech."

Activity 6

Materials: any Unemotional Situation, Sequence, or Rebus Story, Materials Book, pages 56 - 69

Homework: any Unemotional Situation, Sequence, or Rebus Story, Materials Book, pages 56 - 69

Directions: Use forward flowing speech to tell the student, "Remember how we practiced forward flowing speech while imitating the sentences in a story like this? Today, we're going to use them to practice questions and answers. I'll tell you something about the story and then I'll ask you to answer a question. Remember to use forward flowing speech when you answer." Later, reverse the roles.

Have the student tell you or read you part of the story and then ask you a question about that part. To introduce role reversal, tell the student to pretend to be the teacher and ask the questions. Periodically, ask the student to tell you why you are doing this activity. Be sure to reinforce the use of forward flowing speech.

Activity 7

Materials: any commercial card game such as Go Fish® or Rummy® in which questions are included or any set of Memory Cards, Materials Book, pages 43 - 46

Homework: any set of Memory Cards, Materials Book, pages 43 - 46 (Cut apart the pictures and send home with directions on how to play a game similar to Go Fish® or Rummy®.)

Directions: Make three copies and cut apart the pictures. Mix up the cards. Deal five cards to each player. Put the rest in the middle. Use forward flowing speech to tell the student that today you're going to practice forward flowing speech while playing a card game.

Say, "We're going to play a picture card game. See if you have three pictures that match. If you do, put them on the table. I'll do it, too. Now, here's how we play. I'll ask you, 'Do you have a ___?' If you do, give it to me. If not, say 'No. Pick a card.' Then, it will be your turn. We'll take turns until one of us has placed all of our pictures on the table. Before we start, tell me why we're playing this game."

Activity 8

Materials: any object pictures from Matching Pictures, Materials Book, page 31 - 42

Homework: any object pictures from Matching Pictures, Materials Book, page 31 - 42

Directions: Use forward flowing speech to tell the student that today you're going to practice asking each other questions. Place the pictures of the objects in a pile in the middle.

Say, "Here's how we'll practice. Pretend we went to the mall and bought some things. Let's ask each other what we bought. First, I'll say, 'I went to the mall today.' Then, you say, 'What did you buy?' I'll pick a card and say, 'I bought a (whatever the picture is).' Then, it will be your turn. You'll say, 'I went to the mall today.' I'll ask, 'What did you buy?' and you'll pick a picture and say, 'I bought a (whatever the picture is).' Remember to practice forward flowing speech on your turn. I'll use forward flowing speech, too."

35

Vary the carrier sentences and questions such as, "I got a birthday present. What did you get?" "I have to go shopping. What do you need?" or "I received a package. What did you get?"

Activity 9

Materials: Secret Messages 1, 2, 3, or 4, Materials Book, pages 110 - 113

Homework: Secret Messages 1, 2, 3, or 4, Materials Book, pages 110 - 113

Directions: Use forward flowing speech to tell the student you will practice asking and answering questions in forward flowing speech while you decode a secret message.

Say, "Here's how we'll practice. I'll say, 'What letter does this symbol stand for? Where does it go?' You'll answer and then it will be your turn to ask questions about the next symbol. We'll crack the code together. Before we begin, tell me why we're doing this activity."

Activity 10

Materials: 10 - 12 pictures from three or four different sets of Matching Pictures, Materials Book, pages 31 - 42

Homework: 10 - 12 pictures from three or four different sets of Matching Pictures, Materials Book, pages 31 - 42

Directions: Cut apart the pictures. Explain to the student that today you're going to practice asking and answering questions in forward flowing speech while playing a "What is it?" game.

Begin by showing the student the pictures. Take turns naming the pictures in carrier sentences. Then, place the pictures facedown in a pile. Choose a picture and have the student ask questions to try to guess what it is. Model forward flowing speech throughout. Encourage the student to ask category, function, and attribute questions.

Be sure to have the student verbalize why you're playing this game and what the target behaviors are. Also, give a lot of specific verbal feedback (e.g., "I like the way you remembered forward flowing speech on your turn.").

Activity 11

Materials: any Situation Picture, Materials Book, pages 114 - 115

Homework: any Situation Picture, Materials Book, pages 114 - 115

Directions: Cut apart the pictures. Go through the pictures and have the student imitate you as you tell what is happening in the pictures using forward flowing speech. Then, mix up the pictures and place them in a pile in the middle. Explain to the student that you're going to practice forward flowing speech as you ask each other, "What is happening?"

Say, "Here's how we do this activity. I'll pick a card. I'll show it to you and ask, 'What's happening in this picture?' You'll use forward flowing speech to tell me. Then, you get to choose a picture and ask me, 'What's happening?'"

Activity 12

Materials: Thinking Problems 1 or 2, Materials Book, pages 116 - 117

Homework: Thinking Problems 1 or 2, Materials Book, pages 116 - 117

Directions: Cut apart the pictures. Use forward flowing speech to tell the student that today you're going to practice asking questions using forward flowing speech. Go through the pictures and read the problems in forward flowing speech either in imitation or by taking turns. Then, place them in a pile between you.

Say, "This is how we'll practice questions today. You pick a card and say, 'I pick a problem.' I'll ask a question, 'What's the problem?' Then, you answer, 'The problem is *I can't reach the cookie jar*.' Now, it's my turn to pick a card. Before we begin, tell me why we're practicing asking questions."

Activity 13

Materials: What's Your Favorite?, Materials Book, page 118

Homework: What's Your Favorite?, Materials Book, page 118

Directions: When you feel confident that the student can ask questions using forward flowing speech, invite a home or school support person to attend the session. Have the student practice asking the support person some of the "What's Your Favorite . . .?" questions from the activity sheet. If the student is successful, assign him to ask the support person the rest of the questions at home or in the classroom.

This activity (and Activity 14) is difficult and begins transfer (since it takes place outside of therapy and without you being present). Be sure the student and outside support persons realize the difficulty and arrange for the student to attempt the task at a quiet time with no other distractions present (e.g., other people).

Activity 14

Materials: Ask Me Questions, Materials Book, page 119

Homework: Ask Me Questions, Materials Book, page 119

Directions: When you feel confident that the student can answer questions using forward flowing speech, invite a home or school support person to attend the session. Have the student practice answering some of the "Ask Me Questions" when the outside support person asks them. If the student is successful, have him ask the support person to ask the rest of the questions at home or school.

37

Objective 5: The student will produce easy speech using forward flowing speech while formulating one or two sentences within structured activities.

Procedure

During this objective, ask the student to create one or two sentences within the framework of structured activities from Objectives 3 - 4 in which carrier/stereotyped responses and questions and answers were used. You'll also introduce a few new activities. Throughout this objective continue to model forward flowing speech in your directions and on your turns.

Also, continue to review the reason for practicing forward flowing speech in these activities and the target behavior (forward flowing speech). Encourage the student to verbalize the reasons and target behaviors, to self-instruct, and to self-evaluate.

Activity 1

Materials: any set of Matching Pictures, Memory Cards, or Direction Pictures, Materials Book, pages 31 - 42, 43 - 46, or 120 - 121

Homework: any set of Matching Pictures, Memory Cards, or Direction Pictures, Materials Book, pages 31 - 42, 43 - 46, or 120 - 121

Directions: Cut apart the pictures and place them in a pile. Use forward flowing speech to tell the student that today you're going to practice forward flowing speech while creating your own sentences.

Choose a picture and say, "I pick this picture. It's a fish. Fish like to swim in the water." Then, have the student pick a picture, name it, and make up a sentence about it like you did. Be sure to remind the student to use forward flowing speech.

Activity 2

Materials: any set of Matching Pictures or Memory Cards, Materials Book, pages 31 - 42 or 43 - 46

Homework: any set of Matching Pictures or Memory Cards, Materials Book, pages 31 - 42 or 43 - 46

Directions: Use forward flowing speech to tell the student that today you're going to create your own sentences using forward flowing speech.

Make two piles of cards. Select one card from each pile. Then, create a sentence using both words/pictures in the same sentence. Model forward flowing speech. Then, have the student select two cards and create a sentence just like you did. Ask the student what he's supposed to practice while creating the sentence.

For variety, use three or four pictures, but don't create more than one or two sentences. This type of activity will occur in Step 5.

Activity 3

Materials: any two sets of Matching Pictures, Materials Book, pages 31 - 42

Homework: any two sets of Matching Pictures, Materials Book, pages 31 - 42

Directions: Make two copies of the activity sheets and cut apart the pictures from one copy of each sheet.

Ask the student, "Do you remember how we played this game? Today, on your turn, I want you to tell me something about the picture you choose. Let me show you. I'll say, 'I pick a card. I found a space shuttle. I wish I could ride on a space shuttle. Do you need the space shuttle? No. I do.' (Or 'Yes, you do. Here it is.') Now, it's your turn. Remember to practice what kind of talking as we play?"

Be sure to set the game up so you lose. This way you can add comments such as, "Oh well, I lost and you won. I had fun anyway. Maybe someday I'll win."

Activity 4

Materials: any set of Memory Cards, Materials Book, pages 43 - 46

Homework: any set of Memory Cards, Materials Book, pages 43 - 46

Directions: Use forward flowing speech to ask the student, "Do you remember how we played this memory game? Today, I want you to tell me about the pictures you choose. Let me show you. 'I pick a card. I got a zebra. A zebra lives in the zoo. I pick another card. I got a bed. I sleep on a bunk bed. They don't match. Your turn.' When it's your turn, remember to use forward flowing speech."

If possible set up the game so you lose. Make positive competitive remarks when you do.

Activity 5

Materials: any Track Board Game and matching Track Board Sentences, Materials Book, pages 70 - 79

Homework: any Track Board Game and matching Track Board Sentences, Materials Book, pages 70 - 79

Directions: Cut apart the sentences. Use forward flowing speech to ask the student, "Do you remember how we played this game? Today, on our turns, we'll practice forward flowing speech as we make up sentences about the pictures on the sentence cards. I'll show you. I'll say, 'I pick a card. It says, "Here is a motorcycle." You should wear a helmet when you ride a motorcycle. I roll the dice. I can move two spaces. Your turn.' Be sure to make up a sentence and use forward flowing speech."

Remember to set up the game so the student wins. Make positive competitive remarks when you lose.

Activity 6

Materials: any Tic-Tac-Toe Category Board and Tic-Tac-Toe Category Cards, Materials Book, pages 122 - 126

Homework: Tic-Tac-Toe Category Board and any Tic-Tac-Toe Category Cards, Materials Book, pages 122 - 126

Directions: Cut out the Xs and Os and cut apart the category cards. Put the category cards in a pile and place the board so you both can see it. Put the Xs and Os close by.

Tell the student, "Today, we're going to practice forward flowing speech while we name things in categories during a Tic-Tac-Toe game. Here's what we'll say. 'I pick a card. It says, "Name three things you read." I read a book, a magazine, and a letter. I'll put an X here. Your turn.'"

Periodically ask the student to tell you why you're playing this game (*to practice forward flowing speech*) and to tell you what he is to concentrate on (*talking slowly and easily*).

If possible, set up the game so the student wins. Then, make comments such as, "I didn't win today, but maybe I'll win another day," or "I had fun anyway."

Activity 7

Materials: any Situation Picture, Materials Book, pages 114 - 115

Homework: any Situation Picture, Materials Book, pages 114 - 115

Directions: Cut apart the pictures. Put the pictures in front of the student and give him a minute or two to look at them. Then, mix up the pictures and place them facedown in a pile.

Tell the student, "Today, we're going to describe these pictures to each other to see if we can guess what is happening. We can only tell two things. Let me show you. I'll say, 'I pick a card. I see people. I see skates.' Can you guess what is happening in my picture?'" Wait. "Good. Now it's your turn. Remember that we're practicing forward flowing speech so we have to talk slowly and easily."

Activity 8

Materials: What If . . .?, Materials Book, page 127

Homework: What If . . .?, Materials Book, page 127

Directions: Cut apart the pictures and place them in a pile. Use forward flowing speech to tell the student that in this activity the two of you will practice forward flowing speech while reading and creating answers to "What if . . .?" questions.

Take turns asking each other the questions on the activity sheet. Tell the student to answer in just one sentence. Remind him to use forward flowing speech.

Activity 9

Materials: Problem Solving 1, 2, 3, or 4, Materials Book, pages 128 - 131

Homework: Problem Solving 1, 2, 3, or 4, Materials Book, pages 128 - 131

Directions: Show the student the activity sheet. Use forward flowing speech to explain that you'll practice forward flowing speech while reading about the problem and then figuring out the solution.

Say, "Today, we'll practice forward flowing speech. First, we'll read the problem on the top of the sheet. Let's read it together." Read in unison. "Now, let's take turns reading the clues and then telling what to do. I'll show you. 'The first clue says, "Tyrannosaurus Rex is in the middle." I'll write Tyrannosaurus Rex on the middle line. Your turn.' Read the clue and then tell me what you'll do. Remember to use forward flowing speech in your reading and talking."

Activity 10

Materials: Thinking Problems 1 or 2, Materials Book, pages 116 - 117

Homework: Thinking Problems 1 or 2, Materials Book, pages 116 - 117

Directions: Cut apart the pictures. Go through the pictures with the student and take turns reading the problem printed on the picture using forward flowing speech. Then, mix up the problems and place them in a pile.

Tell the student that you will take turns asking each other how to solve the problems. Say, "This is how we'll practice forward flowing speech today. Pick a picture and read me the problem. Then, ask me, 'What can I do?' I'll answer in forward flowing speech. I'll say, 'I can climb on a chair.' Then, I'll say, 'Your turn.' Be sure to use forward flowing speech when you solve my problem."

Remember to reinforce the student for using forward flowing speech by saying, "I liked the way you used slow, forward flowing speech in your answer."

Activity 11

Materials: What's Wrong? 1, 2, 3, or 4, Materials Book, pages 132 - 135

Homework: What's Wrong? 1, 2, 3, 4, Materials Book, pages 132 - 135

Directions: Use forward flowing speech to tell the student, "Today, we're going to practice forward flowing speech while we tell each other what is wrong in the picture. Here's how we'll do it. We'll each look for something that is wrong. Then, we'll take turns telling each other what is wrong. I'll start, 'I found something that is wrong.' You ask me, 'What did you find?' I'll answer, 'I found a horse with no tail. Your turn.'"

Periodically, ask the student to tell you why you're doing this activity (*to practice easy talking*) and what the target behaviors are (*slow and forward flowing speech*). Also, have the student self-evaluate by asking, "Are you remembering to use forward flowing speech?"

Path 2

> **Goal 3.2:** **The student will produce easy speech in structured activities by modifying speech production through word-initiation techniques.**

If you've selected this path for Step 3, you'll be addressing the motor component of speech production by teaching the student to modify how she initiates production of words by using bouncing, sliding, light contacts, and easy onsets. You should model forward flowing speech even though it won't be addressed directly so that the student also hears a model of slow rate and continuous phonation.

Linguistic components and psychosocial components will be addressed in the same manner as in Path 1. Similarly, you'll continue to enlist the student's participation in order to develop positive attitudes and self-advocacy.

For some students, once easy ways to initiate words are learned, stuttering will decrease significantly and it will be possible to gradually fade out the techniques. For other students, the use of the techniques may remain optional for cancellations, pull-outs, or preparatory sets throughout the program. If the emphasis is on learning easy speech production, however, either way will result in a successful completion of the program.

Before beginning the actual practice of the techniques, it may be helpful to review Steps to Easy Speech, Materials Book, page 10, so the student will understand the purpose of this step as well as recognize the progress being made toward the final goal.

What if the student has trouble producing the modification? Encourage the student to produce it in unison with you at a very slow rate.

What if the student inserts a schwa into bouncing? Remind the student to produce the consonant and vowel of the word as a way of easing into the word. Don't allow the student to repeat only the consonant.

What if the student gets into a rhythm of bounces? Encourage the student to vary the number of bounces.

What if the student stops after each bounce? Remind the student that the sound has to keep going all the time. Show the student the differences using the examples on Rules, Materials Book, page 137.

What if the student gets stuck on the consonant in a slide? Encourage the student to move forward into the following consonant or vowel. Demonstrate how to do this.

What if the student is tense during the techniques? Encourage the student to produce the techniques slowly and easily. Consider introducing some of the relaxation exercises in the Materials Book, page 17.

What if the student has trouble initiating the easy onset or light contact? Remind the student to take air in and then begin to let it out before bringing the vocal folds or articulators together.

What if the student has trouble as you introduce the next higher level of response (e.g., you move from carrier sentences to questions and answers)? Drop back to the lower level response until you secure success. Then, reintroduce the higher level response. Have the student try the response type in unison or imitation before trying it on her own.

What if the student stutters while formulating? Let the student finish and then repeat the sentence

42

using word-initiation techniques on the stuttered words. Ask the student to imitate your production. If the student has many disfluencies, return to an earlier objective and then try formulative tasks again at a later date.

What if the student formulates too much (e.g., begins conversing or gives more than one or two sentences)? Remind the student that you have to progress in small steps. Right now the purpose is to formulate only one or two sentences. Let the student know that soon you'll work on conversation. Review Steps to Easy Speech, Materials Book, page 10, to show the student the need to take things "one step at a time." Remind the student of the need to practice the new way of talking many times so it becomes a firm habit. Relate the practice to learning any motor act such as playing an instrument or learning to play a sport.

What if the student (or the family/teachers) expresses concern over continued difficulty in conversation? Remind them that you don't expect transfer to real-life situations until much later in the program. Review Steps to Easy Speech, Materials Book, page 10, and show them how continuous progress is occurring, but not to expect transfer yet.

What if the student has sound-specific difficulties? Spend extra time working on activities focusing on the use of word-initiation techniques on words beginning with the difficult sounds. For example, if the student has difficulty with /s/, select several /s/ words and model how to use different word-initiation techniques on them (e.g., bouncing, sliding, light contact). Have the student use the techniques on the words in unison with you and then in imitation. Focus on moving forward through the word.

Attitudes/Advocacy

Stress attitudes such as:

- When I use a word initiating modification, I am taking control.
- I'm replacing old habits of hard talking with new habits of easy talking.
- I can't stutter and control at the same time, so I'll choose to control.

Be sure to have the student define and describe the techniques being learned for you and others you invite to the sessions in "I" terms (e.g., "I'm using bouncing.") Also, stress good sportsmanship by modeling attitudes such as, "It's fun to play even if you don't win, Maybe I'll win another day," and "No one wins all the time."

If you know an older student or adult who uses word-initiation techniques, you might invite that person to join a session so that the student sees how effective the techniques can be and so the student realizes that she's not alone in working on speech production.

Suggestions for Support Providers

Home and School

Share Home and School Letters 3.2A, Materials Book, pages 156 - 157, which describe the word-initiation techniques and Home and School Letters 3.2B, Materials Book, pages 158 - 159, which describe cancellations, pull-outs, and preparatory sets. Invite parents/significant others and teachers to attend a session and have the student demonstrate the word-initiation techniques for them.

Send home activities which the student has successfully completed in therapy for the student to practice with the parents/significant others. Be sure to include directions so the support people know what to do and what to expect the student to do.

Ask the teacher if you can have a copy of the student's books so you can incorporate vocabulary and topics being covered in the classroom into your activities. Talk with the teacher about situations in which the student might use the techniques with her in the classroom. Practice some tasks from What's Your Favorite...? and Ask Me Questions, Materials Book, pages 118 - 119, with the teacher in the therapy session and then assign the rest for outside practice. Have the student and teacher select practice times that will be relatively stress free (e.g., at quiet times when no one else is present).

Objective 1: The student will be introduced to word-initiation techniques of bouncing, sliding, light contacts, and easy onsets.

Procedure

Introduce each modification in the order presented below. Generally, you'll need one day to introduce the concept of word-initiation modification and the rules for bouncing. On the second day, review bouncing and introduce sliding. On the third day, review bouncing and sliding and then introduce light contacts and easy onsets together. Of course, you may spend more time on each technique if desired. Once the techniques have been introduced, practice using them in structured activities throughout the remaining objectives.

Bouncing
When introducing bouncing, define and describe the technique. Model how to bounce, being sure to do so slowly and with continuous phonation. Be sure to vary the number of "bounces" to insure the student is developing control. Discuss the value of bouncing (e.g., doing what you dislike) as well as its differences from repeating (e.g., it's slow, relaxed, and controlled). Also, remind the student that bouncing can be used on almost any word, making it a very useful technique. Encourage the student to describe the technique (e.g., "When I bounce, I repeat the beginning of the word in a slow easy way.")

Sliding
When introducing sliding, describe the technique. Model how to slide in a slow relaxed manner. Discuss the value of sliding and the words upon which it may be helpful. Encourage the student to describe the technique (e.g., "When I slide, I stretch out the beginning sound of a word and ease into the next sound"). Be sure to have the student verbalize those words on which a slide can't be used — stops and affricates.

Light contacts and easy onsets
These can be introduced separately or together, but usually introducing them together is easier if time permits. Discuss how together these two techniques allow the student to modify any word. Encourage the student to describe the techniques (e.g., "When I use an easy onset, I bring my vocal folds together easily; when I use a light contact, I bring my speech helpers together easily").

44

Activity 1

Materials: Introducing Word-initiation Techniques, Materials Book, page 136

Homework: Introducing Word-initiation Techniques, Materials Book, page 136

Directions: Tell the student that it's time to learn some other ways of easy speaking. These involve starting words in an easy way. Go over the activity sheet and define and demonstrate each technique.

Explain the differences between bouncing (a type of easy speech that involves easy disfluencies) and part-word repetitions (a type of hard speech or stuttering). Say, "You might think bouncing is the same as part-word repetition. In some ways it is. In bouncing we do repeat part of a word. It's different, though, because it's relaxed and effortless and we do it on purpose. At first, we'll vary the number of bounces. Usually we'll bounce 1, 2, or 3 times, but we could bounce 10 times if we wanted to. The important thing to remember is to bounce slowly and easily and to keep the sound going. We want to keep moving forward."

You'll also want to explain the difference between sliding and prolongations. Say, "Sliding might seem like a prolongation, but it's different. Prolongations are long and tense and we don't want to do them. Slides are easy and relaxed and we do them on purpose to ease into a word. We'll vary the length of our slides, but we'll always make them move easily into the next sound."

Review the Analysis of Disfluencies Chart, Materials Book, page 13, on which you listed bouncing, sliding, light contacts, and easy onsets on the side with easy disfluencies. Tell the student that you'll start by learning bouncing. Then, the next day you'll learn sliding and review bouncing. Then, the third day you'll learn easy onsets and light contacts. After that you can practice all the ways to modify how you start (initiate) a word so that your speech will be easy and relaxed.

Activity 2

Materials: Bouncing Rules and Bouncing Practice 1 and 2, Materials Book, pages 137 - 139

Homework: Bouncing Rules and Bouncing Practice 1 and 2, Materials Book, pages 137 - 139

Directions: Tell the student that you're going to begin by learning bouncing. Go over the rules for bouncing and demonstrate how to bounce. Have the student say the practice words on the Bouncing Rules activity sheet with you in unison. Then, using bouncing, tell the student that you can practice bouncing in reading and in talking. Follow the directions on the Bouncing Practice activity sheet. Tell the student, "I'll read each word or sentence (or name or describe each picture) two times. I'll bounce on some of the words. Listen the first time. Then, repeat the sentence with me the second time. Be sure to bounce on the words just like I do." Do NOT bounce on every word. If the student does well, repeat the activity sheets taking turns being sure to use bouncing.

Activity 3

Materials: Sliding Rules and Sliding Practice 1 and 2, Materials Book, pages 140 - 142

Homework: Sliding Rules and Sliding Practice 1 and 2, Materials Book, pages 140 - 142

Directions: Before introducing sliding, review the word-initiation technique of bouncing. Have the student practice bouncing in imitation using any activity from Objective 2. Then, tell the student, "Today we're going to learn another way to use easy speech when we start words. Today we'll practice sliding. Remember how we learned what sliding was in our last session?" Go over the Sliding Rules activity sheet. Be sure to model sliding as you complete the activity sheet.

Then, go over the Sliding Practice 1 or 2 activity sheet. Tell the student, "I'll read these words and sentences (or name and describe these pictures) two times using sliding. Listen the first time and then join me the second time. Be sure to use sliding just like I do." Remember you can only slide on words that begin with vowels or continuant consonants. If the student does well, repeat the activity sheets taking turns being sure to use sliding.

Activity 4

Materials: Light Contact and Easy Onset Rules, Speech Articulators, and Light Contact and Easy Onset Practice 1 and 2, Materials Book, pages 143. 144 and 145-146

Homework: Light Contact and Easy Onset Rules, Speech Articulators, and Light Contact and Easy Onset Practice 1 and 2, Materials Book, pages 143. 144 and 145-146

Directions: Before beginning this session, review the word-initiation techniques of bouncing and sliding and practice them in any imitative activities from Objective 2. Then, tell the student, "We have two other word-initiation techniques to learn to use when we want to talk in easy speech. They're very similar. They are light contacts and easy onsets."

Use the Light Contact and Easy Onset Rules activity sheet and the Speech Articulators activity sheet to teach the techniques. Then, tell the student, "Now, we need to practice light contacts and easy onsets." Model light contacts and easy onsets as you complete the practice worksheets. Say, "I'll read these words and sentences (or name and describe these pictures) two times. Listen the first time and then join me in using light contacts or easy onsets the second time." If the student does well, repeat the activity sheets taking turns.

When you finish this session, tell the student, "Now, we're going to practice easy speech by using bouncing, sliding, light contacts, and easy onsets in a lot of different activities and games." Move on to Objective 2.

Objective 2: The student will produce easy speech by imitating word-initiation techniques of bouncing, sliding, light contacts, and easy onsets in structured activities.

Procedure

In this objective, have the student imitate the word-initiation techniques in a variety of activities. Model the techniques in your speech both during the activities and during directions and conversation. Also, remember to speak a little slower and to use forward flowing speech (run your words together) even though these behaviors are not being addressed directly in this path to easy speech.

Be sure to give the student opportunities to verbalize the purpose of the practice and the target behaviors. Encourage the student to describe the techniques and the rules for how and when to use them from time to time. Reinforce the student by telling her, "I liked the way you used (bouncing) on that word." Also, have the student self-evaluate from time to time by asking, "How do you think you did in that activity?" Involve the student by having her select words on which to practice and the technique to use on the words selected.

Activity 1

Materials: any pictures from Matching Pictures or Memory Cards, Materials Book, pages 31 - 46

Homework: none

Directions: Show the student the pictures one at a time. Say, "I'm going to name and describe these pictures using our word-initiation techniques. You say them after me using whatever technique I used, just like I did. Listen, 'Pepepencil.' You say that." Wait. "'F——ish.' You say that." Wait. After the student catches on, drop the "You say that" cue. Vary the word-initiation techniques you model. Progress from words to phrases, carrier sentences (e.g., "I s—-ee a pepepencil."), and descriptive sentences (e.g., "The fififish is [light contact] gold.").

Activity 2

Materials: any age-appropriate Reading Practice activity sheet, Materials Book, pages 47 -55

Homework: none

Directions: Point to a word, model any word-initiation technique, and have the student imitate your production. Progress to the phrases and sentences. Be sure to tell the student why you're doing these tasks (e.g., to learn to talk in easy speech) and what the target behaviors are (e.g., bouncing, sliding, light contacts, and easy onsets).

Variation 1: For more practice, use any Reading Practice activity sheet, and underline words on which to practice the desired technique. If bouncing, you might also have the student place a number over the word to indicate the number of bounces to be used. To involve the student, have her select the words to be underlined.

Variation 2: Once the student has practiced techniques individually, use any reading worksheet to combine practice of the techniques using the procedure of underlining, but add a letter above the word to indicate which technique to practice (e.g., B = bouncing; S = sliding; EO = easy onsets; and LC = light contacts).

Activity 3

Materials: any Unemotional Situation, Sequence, or Rebus Story, Materials Book, pages 56 - 69

Homework: none

Directions: Tell the student, "I'm going to read this story. I'll use some of our word-initiation techniques. After I finish each sentence, I want you to repeat it just like I did. Remember to include bouncing, sliding, light contacts, and easy onsets just like I did."

> **Objective 3:** The student will produce easy speech by using word-initiation techniques of bouncing, sliding, light contacts, and easy onsets in carrier/stereotyped responses in structured activities.

Procedure

Introduce a variety of activities in which the student can practice word-initiation techniques while saying stereotyped sentences (e.g., "I pick a card, I found a piece, I want a picture, It goes here, I put it right here, Your turn.") and carrier sentences (e.g., "I found a ___, This is a ___, I need a ___, I have a ___.").

Some activities will have a game format. If at all possible, arrange the activity so the student will win as you want to build confidence in this step. Learning to remain fluent while dealing with competition comes in the next step. To prepare the student for losing, model good sportsmanship by saying things such as, "Oh well, I had fun anyway. It's fun to play even if you don't win. Maybe I'll win another day."

When introducing a new activity with unfamiliar vocabulary, review the new words in imitation first. Tell the student, "Let's practice our word-initiation techniques in imitation before we begin this activity." Periodically, ask the student, "Why are we doing these activities?" Stress that it takes a lot of practice to learn new habits. Be sure to have the student self-evaluate from time to time also by asking, "How did you do?"

Activity 1

Materials: any set of Matching Pictures, Materials Book, pages 31 - 42.

Homework: any set of Matching Pictures, Materials Book, pages 31 - 42

Directions: Make two copies of two different boards. Cut apart the pictures from one copy of each board. If you think any of the words may be difficult or unfamiliar, go through them first and have the student imitate you as you say the words individually or in carrier sentences using the different word-initiation techniques. Place a board in front of you and another in front of the student. Mix up the pictures and place in a stack between you. Be sure one of your pictures is on the bottom so the student wins. Model positive statements about losing.

Model bouncing, sliding, light contacts, and easy onsets as you introduce the game by saying, "Now, we're going to practice bouncing, sliding, light contacts, and easy onsets in some games. We'll use simple sentences over and over so it will be easy for you to concentrate on your forward flowing speech. On each turn we'll say, 'I pick a card. I found a ___. I need/don't need it. Your turn.' Remember to include some bouncing, sliding, light contacts, and easy onsets on your turn."

Periodically, ask the student to verbalize why you're playing the game (e.g., to practice easy speech), and what you're to do (e.g., use bouncing, sliding, light contacts, and easy onsets).

Activity 2

Materials: any Memory Cards, Materials Book, pages 43 - 46

Homework: any Memory Cards, Materials Book, pages 43 - 46

Directions: Make two copies and cut the pictures apart. If you think any of the words may be difficult or unfamiliar, have the student imitate you as you say them individually or in carrier sentences.

Then, play a memory game using the pictures. Place the pictures upside down between you and the student. Model word-initiation techniques as you say, "Now, we're going to practice bouncing, sliding, light contacts, and easy onsets while playing a memory game. We'll use short simple sentences so you can concentrate on your easy speech. On each turn we'll say, 'I pick a card. It's a ___. I pick another card. It's a ___. They do/do not match.' If they match, you get another turn. If not, turn the pictures upside-down again and say, 'Your turn.'"

Include the techniques in your directions. If possible, let the student win. Be sure to model positive statements about losing such as, "I had fun even though I didn't win."

Activity 3

Materials: any commercial board game or any Track Board Game and Track Board Sentences, Materials Book, pages 70 - 79; game markers and a spinner or die

Homework: any Track Board Game and matching Track Board Sentences, Materials Book, pages 70 - 79

Directions: Cut apart the Track Board Sentences. If you think any of the words may be difficult or unfamiliar, have the student imitate you as you say them individually or in carrier sentences. Then, tell the student that you're going to practice bouncing, sliding, light contacts, and easy onsets in simple sentences while playing a track board game.

Place the game board between you and the student. Place the Track Board Sentences in a pile to the side. Before each turn you'll select a Track Board Sentence and use bouncing, sliding, light contacts, or easy onsets while saying, "I pick a sentence. It says, 'Here is a car.' Now, I spin the spinner (or roll the die). I got a 4. I can move 4 spaces. Your turn." If a player lands on a space with a message, the player should read the message and incorporate some bouncing, sliding, light contacts, and easy onsets.

If possible, set up the game so the student wins. Model positive statements such as, "I didn't win today, but I still had fun. It's fun to play even when you don't win. Maybe I'll win the next time."

Periodically, ask the student to verbalize why you're playing the game and what the target behaviors are. As you play, be sure to reinforce the student by saying, "I like the way you're using (bouncing, sliding, light contacts, or easy onsets) in your sentences. Also, occasionally ask the student to comment on how she is doing.

Activity 4

Materials: any Opposite Association Pictures or Words, Materials Book, pages 80 - 85; pencil

Homework: any Opposite Association Pictures or Words, Materials Book, pages 80 - 85

Directions: Have the student imitate your word-initiation techniques as you name the opposites. Then, model the word-initiation techniques as you tell the student, "Today, we're going to practice bouncing, sliding, light contacts, and easy onsets in simple sentences while we find opposites. Here's what we'll say, 'This is a ____. The opposite of ____ is ____. Here is a ____. They go together. I'll draw a line between them. Your turn.'" Be sure to include the techniques in your directions. Ask the student to tell you what kind of talking she'll use.

Activity 5

Materials: any Bingo Function Board and Cards, Materials Book, pages 86 - 90; circles

Homework: any Bingo Function Board and Cards, Materials Book, pages 86 - 90

Directions: Cut apart the cards and circles. Use word-initiation techniques as you read the Bingo Function Cards and have the student imitate you. Then, give each player a Bingo Function Board. Place the cards in a pile in the middle and put the circles to the side. Tell the student, "Today we're going to play a game using simple sentences so you can practice bouncing, sliding, easy onsets, and light contacts. The game is like Bingo®. I'll go first and show you how to play. 'I pick a card. It says, "something you stir with." That's a spoon. I found it on my board. I put a circle on it. Your turn.' You should put a circle on the spoon on your board, too. We'll see who gets five circles in a row first (down, across, or diagonally)."

Periodically, ask the student to tell you why you're playing the game and what the target behaviors are. Reinforce the student by saying, "I like the way you used (bouncing, sliding, light contacts, or easy onsets) on your turn."

Activity 6

Materials: any Hidden Picture and its Hidden Picture Objects and Words companion activity sheet, Materials Book, pages 91 - 98

Homework: any Hidden Picture and its Hidden Picture Objects and Words companion activity sheet, Materials Book, pages 91 - 98

Directions: Cut out the companion words or pictures. Use the pictures for younger students and the words for older students. If you think the words may be difficult or unfamiliar, have the student imitate you as you name them or use them in carrier sentences. Place the hidden picture on the table and the accompanying pictures or words in a pile.

Model the word-initiation techniques as you tell the student, "Today, we'll practice bouncing, sliding, light contacts, and easy onsets while we hunt for hidden objects. I'll show you how we play. I'll say, 'I pick a picture (word). It is ____. I'm looking for ____. I found it. Your turn.' Remember, we're doing this to practice what kind of talking?" Be sure to reinforce the student by saying, "I like the way you used (bouncing, sliding, light contacts, or easy onsets) on that turn."

Activity 7

Materials: any Word Puzzle, Materials Book, pages 99 - 102

Homework: any Word Puzzle and words/pictures, Materials Book, pages 99 - 102

Directions: Cut out the word and pictures and put them in a pile. If you think any of the words may be difficult or unfamiliar, have the student imitate you as you name them individually or in carrier sentences. Place a word puzzle on the table. Put the words/pictures in a pile.

Model word-initiation techniques as you tell the student, "Today, we're going to practice bouncing, sliding, light contacts, and easy onsets as we do a word puzzle. We'll say, 'I pick a card. It is a (says) ____. I'm looking for ____. I found it. It goes down. Your turn.' The words can go up, down, across, backwards, or diagonally." Remember to include the word-initiation techniques in your directions and conversation.

Activity 8

Materials: Message Guessing 1 and 2, Materials Book, pages 103 - 104

Homework: Have the student create an original message for you to guess next time.

Directions: Cut apart the messages. Use a pencil, chips, or circles from the Bingo Function Boards, Materials Book, pages 86 - 89, to mark the letters chosen and the number of guesses. Place the Message Guessing message in front of the student. Lay out Message Guessing 2 nearby.

Model word-initiation techniques as you introduce the activity. Tell the student, "Today, we'll practice bouncing, sliding, light contacts, and easy onsets while trying to figure out this message. You'll guess letters and if they're in the message, I'll fill them in. You should mark the letters you choose on this sheet because you only get 15 guesses. You can guess the message any time you think you know it. On each turn say, 'I want the letter ____.' When you want to guess, say, 'I want to guess the message. It says, ____.' Now, before we start, tell me why we're playing this game."

> **Objective 4:** The student will produce easy speech by using word-initiation techniques of bouncing, sliding, light contacts, and easy onsets while asking and answering questions in structured tasks.

Procedure

Model word-initiation techniques during questions and answers of structured activities. Many of the activities will be the same as in Objective 3, but with the addition of questions and answers. Some new activities will also be added. If you feel the words may be difficult or unfamiliar, begin by having the student imitate your production of the words individually or in carrier sentences before beginning the question/answer activity. In some instances, it will be necessary to reverse roles so the student can ask the questions. In other activities, the questions are inherent in the game/activity.

Activity 1

Materials: any two sets of Matching Pictures, Materials Book, pages 31 - 42

Homework: any two sets of Matching Pictures, Materials Book, pages 31 - 42

Directions: Make two copies of two different boards. Cut apart the pictures from one copy of each board. Tell the student that you're going to incorporate questions and answers into your practice. Follow directions for this activity from Objective 3, but change the directions as follows: "Today, we'll say, 'I pick a card. I found a ____. Do you need it?'" Wait. If the answer is "No," continue. "Do I need it? Yes I do. Now it's your turn."

Model bouncing, sliding, light contacts, and easy onsets throughout your turn and remind the student to use them as needed. Reinforce the student for using the modifications and ask the student to self-evaluate (e.g., "Did you remember to use bouncing, sliding, light contacts, and easy onsets?"). Be sure to ask for self-evaluation when the student has succeeded so that the approach is a positive one.

Activity 2

Materials: none

Homework: none (You might tell the student to play the "I'm Thinking of . . ." game at home or with friends.)

Directions: Model forward flowing speech as you describe the following activity. Tell the student, "Today we're going to practice bouncing, sliding, light contacts, and easy onsets during an 'I'm Thinking of...' activity. Here's what we do. You think of something in the room, but don't tell me what it is. Now, I'll ask you questions to see if I can guess what it is. If I can't guess what it is after 10 questions, you'll have to tell me the answer. I'll use bouncing, sliding, light contacts, and easy onsets when I ask my questions. I'll start with, 'What is it made of?' After I guess, then it will be your turn to ask me questions about what I'm thinking of. Don't forget to modify your speech."

Activity 3

Materials: any Who's Guilty? activity sheet, Materials Book, pages 105 - 106; pencil

Homework: any Who's Guilty? activity sheet Materials Book, pages 105 - 106

Directions: Tell the student that today you'll practice bouncing, sliding, light contacts, and easy onsets while playing Who's Guilty? Show the student the Who's Guilty? activity sheet. Tell the student to pick a person or animal on the sheet. Say, "That person/animal is guilty of a crime and I have to guess which one it is. I'll remember to use bouncing, sliding, light contacts and easy onsets when I ask questions to try to figure out the guilty party. The questions have to be ones you can answer with a *yes* or *no*." To help, use a pencil or circles from the Bingo Function Boards, Materials Book, pages 86 - 89, to mark those pictures that you eliminate. Review with the student why you're playing this game and which techniques you're practicing.

Note: If the student has trouble asking questions that reduce the number of possibilities (e.g., she asks questions specific to a picture such as, "Is it the bat?"), model questions related to categories (e.g., "Is it a boy? Does the animal have two legs?").

Activity 4

Materials: any 20 Matching Pictures, Materials Book, pages 31 - 42

Homework: any 20 Matching Pictures, Materials Book, pages 31 - 42

Directions: Cut the pictures apart. Place the 20 pictures on the table facing up. Tell the student, "Today, we're going to play Ten Questions. We can practice bouncing, sliding, light contacts, and easy onsets while we play. In this game, I'll think of one of these pictures. You have to ask questions to figure out which one I'm thinking of. You have 10 questions and then you have to guess. You can guess sooner if you figure it out sooner. You can only ask questions that I can answer with a *yes* or *no*. I want you to use bouncing, sliding, light contacts, and easy onsets when you ask the questions. I'll show you how. You think of a picture and I'll ask the questions. Then, it will be your turn." Remember to model the word-initiation techniques as you give the directions and on your turn.

Note: If you select pictures within only one or two categories, most questions will relate to descriptions. If you mix pictures from several categories, you can model questions related to categories and functions as well.

Activity 5

Materials: any Riddles, Materials Book, pages 107 - 109

Homework: any Riddles, Materials Book, pages 107 - 109

Directions: Cut apart the riddles. Use word-initiation techniques as you tell the student, "Today, we're going to practice bouncing, sliding, light contacts, and easy onsets in questions while we ask each other riddles." Give the student the cards and say, "Here's a pile of riddles. Let's go through them first and pick out some words we can practice on." Underline words and place a letter cue over them (B = bounce; S - slide; LC = light contact; and EO = easy onset). Then, say, "I'll take the first one and read the riddle. See if you can answer it. Use bouncing, sliding, light contacts, and easy onsets in your answer." After your turn, say, "Now you pick a riddle and read it to me."

Activity 6

Materials: any Unemotional Situation, Rebus, or Sequence Story, Materials Book, pages 56 - 69

Homework: any Unemotional Situation, Rebus or Sequence Story, Materials Book, pages 56 - 69

Directions: Using word-initiation techniques, tell the student, "Remember how we practiced our word-initiation techniques while imitating the sentences in this story? Today, we're going to use them to practice questions and answers. I'll tell you something about the story and then I'll ask you to answer a question. Remember to use bouncing, sliding, light contacts, or easy onsets when you answer."

Later, reverse the roles. Have the student tell you or read you part of the story and then ask you a question about that part. To introduce the role reversal, tell the student to pretend to be the teacher and ask the questions. Periodically, ask the student to tell you why you're doing this activity. Be sure to reinforce the use of the word-initiation techniques.

Activity 7

Materials: any commercial card game such as Go Fish® or Rummy® in which questions are included or any Memory Cards, Materials Book, pages 43 - 46

Homework: any Memory Cards, Materials Book, pages 43 - 46. (Make three copies. Cut the pictures apart. Send home with directions on how to play a game similar to Go Fish® or Rummy®.)

Directions: Make three copies and cut apart the pictures. Mix up the cards. Deal five cards to each player. Put the rest in the middle. Using word-initiation techniques, tell the student that today you're going to practice bouncing, sliding, light contacts and easy onsets while playing a card game. Say, "We're going to play a picture card game. See if you have three pictures that match. If you do, put them on the table. I'll do that, too."

When you're finished, say, "Now, here's how we play. I'll ask you, 'Do you have a ___?' If you do, you give it to me. If not, you say 'No. Pick a card.' Then, it will be your turn. We'll take turns until one of us has placed all of our pictures on the table. Before we start, tell me why we're playing this game and what we're practicing."

Activity 8

Materials: any object pictures from Matching Pictures and/or Direction pictures, Materials Book, pages 31 - 42 and 120 - 121

Homework: any object pictures from Matching Pictures and/or Direction Pictures, Materials Book, pages 31 and 120 - 121

Directions: Using word-initiation techniques, tell the student that today you're going to practice asking each other questions. Place the pictures of the objects in a pile in the middle. Say, "Here's how we'll practice. We'll pretend we went to a mall and bought some things. We'll ask each other what we bought. First, I'll say, 'I went to the mall today.' Then, you say, 'What did you buy?' I'll pick a card and say, 'I bought a (name of picture).'"

"Then, it will be your turn. You'll say, 'I went to the mall today.' I'll ask, 'What did you buy?' and you'll pick a picture and say, 'I bought a (name of picture).' Remember to practice bouncing, sliding, light contacts, and easy onsets when you name the pictures. You can also use them on other words in the sentence if you want to. I'll use them on my turn, too."

54

(If using the Direction Pictures, change the routine to, "I'm going on vacation." "What will you see?" "I'll see a (name of picture).")

Note: Vary the carrier sentences and questions in a number of ways. For example:

> I got a birthday present. What did you get?
> I have to go shopping. What do you need?
> I received a package. What did you get?

Activity 9

Materials: any Secret Messages, Materials Book, pages 110 - 113

Homework: any Secret Messages, Materials Book, pages 110 - 113

Directions: Using word-initiation techniques, tell the student you'll practice asking and answering questions using bouncing, sliding, light contacts, and easy onsets while you decode a secret message. Say, "I'll say 'What letter does this symbol stand for? Where does it go?' Then, it will be your turn to ask the questions about the next symbol. We'll crack the code together, but first, why are we doing this activity?"

Activity 10

Materials: 10 to 12 pictures from several sets of Matching Pictures, Materials Book, pages 31 - 42

Homework: 10 to 12 pictures from several sets of Matching Pictures, Materials Book, pages 31 - 42

Directions: Cut apart the pictures. Tell the student that today you're going to practice bouncing, sliding, light contacts, and easy onsets as you ask and answer questions while playing a "What is it?" game. Begin by showing the student the pictures. Take turns naming the pictures in carrier sentences. Then, place the pictures facedown in a pile. Select a picture and have the other person ask questions to try to guess what it is.

Model word-initiation techniques throughout. Encourage the student to ask category, function, and attribute questions. Be sure to have the student verbalize why you're playing this game and what the target behaviors are. Also, give a lot of specific verbal feedback (e.g., "I like the way you remembered to use [bouncing, sliding, light contacts and/or easy onsets] on your turn.").

Activity 11

Materials: any Situation Pictures, Materials Book, pages 114 - 115

Homework: any Situation Pictures, Materials Book, pages 114 - 115

Directions: Cut apart the pictures. Go through the situation pictures and tell the student to imitate you as you tell what is happening in the pictures using word-initiation techniques. Then, mix up the pictures and place them in a pile in the middle. Tell the student that you're going to practice bouncing, sliding, light contacts, and easy onsets as you ask each other, "What is happening?"

Say, "Here's how we do this activity. I pick a card. I show it to you and ask, 'What's happening in this picture?' Then, you use bouncing, sliding, light contacts, or easy onsets to tell me. Then, you get to pick a picture and ask me 'What's happening?'"

Activity 12

Materials: any Thinking Problems, Materials Book, pages 116 - 117

Homework: any Thinking Problems, Materials Book, pages 116 - 117

Directions: Cut apart the problems. Using word-initiation techniques, tell the student that today you're going to practice asking questions with bouncing, sliding, light contacts, and easy onsets.

First, go through the Thinking Problems pictures and use bouncing, sliding, light contacts, and easy onsets as you read the problem either in imitation or taking turns. Then, place the cards in a pile between you. Say, "This is how we'll practice questions today. You pick a card and say, 'I pick a problem.' Next, I'll ask a question, 'What's the problem?' Then, you answer, 'The problem is I can't reach the cookie jar.' Now, it's my turn to pick a card. Before I do, tell me why we practice these questions."

Activity 13

Materials: What's Your Favorite . . .?, Materials Book, page 118

Homework: What's Your Favorite . . .?, Materials Book, page 118

Directions: When you feel confident that the student can ask questions using word-initiation techniques with you, invite a home or school support person to attend the session and have the student practice asking the support person some of the "What's Your Favorite . . .?" questions from the activity sheet. If the student is successful, assign her to ask the support person the rest of the questions at home or in the classroom.

Note: This is difficult and really begins transfer. Be sure the student and outside support persons realize the difficulty and arrange for the student to attempt the task at a quiet time with no other distractions present (e.g., other people).

Activity 14

Materials: Ask Me Questions, Materials Book, page 119

Homework: Ask Me Questions, Materials Book, page 119

Directions: When you feel confident that the student can answer questions using word-initiation techniques with you, invite a home or school support person to attend the session and ask the student some of the "Ask Me" questions. If the student is successful answering these questions, have her ask the support person to ask the rest of the questions at home or school.

Note: This is difficult and really begins transfer. Be sure the student and outside support persons realize the difficulty and arrange for the student to attempt the task at a quiet time with no other distractions present (e.g., other people).

Objective 5: The student will produce easy speech by using word-initiation techniques of bouncing, sliding, light contacts, and easy onsets while formulating words, phrases, and sentences within structured activities.

Procedure

During this objective, the student practices word-initiation techniques of bouncing, sliding, easy onsets, and light contacts while formulating words, phrases, and one or two sentences within structured tasks. Model the word-initiation techniques when giving directions, during the activities, and during conversation.

Continue to review the reason for practicing word-initiation techniques in these activities and the target behaviors (e.g., bouncing, sliding, light contacts, and easy onsets). Encourage the student to verbalize the reasons and target behaviors, to self-instruct, and to self-evaluate.

Activity 1

Materials: any Matching Pictures, Memory Cards, or Direction Pictures, Materials Book, pages 31 - 46, and 120 - 121

Homework: any Matching Pictures, Memory Cards, or Direction Pictures, Materials Book, pages 31 - 46, and 120 - 121

Directions: Cut apart the pictures. Using word-initiation techniques, tell the student that today you're going to practice bouncing, sliding, light contacts, and easy onsets while creating your own sentences. Place the pictures in a pile. Select a picture and say, "I pick this picture. It's a fish. Fish like to swim in the water."

Then, tell the student to pick a picture, name it, and then make up a sentence about it just like you did. Be sure to remind the student to use the target behaviors.

Activity 2

Materials: any Matching Pictures, Memory Cards, or Direction Pictures, Materials Book, pages 31 - 46, and 120 - 121

Homework: any Matching Pictures, Memory Cards, or Direction Pictures, Materials Book, pages 31 - 46, and 120 - 121

Directions: Using word-initiation techniques, tell the student that today you're going to create your own sentences using bouncing, sliding, light contacts, and easy onsets. Make two piles of cards. Select one from each pile. Then, create a sentence using both words in the same sentence. Model bouncing, sliding, light contacts, and easy onsets. Tell the student to select two pictures and create a sentence just like you did. Ask the student what she's supposed to practice while creating the sentence.

For variety, use three or four pictures, but only create one or two sentences, not a whole story. The student will practice this type of activity in Step 5, Transfer.

Activity 3

Materials: any two sets of Matching Pictures, Materials Book, pages 31 - 42

Homework: any two sets of Matching Pictures, Materials Book, pages 31 - 42

Directions: Make two copies. Cut apart the pictures from one copy of each activity sheet. Tell the student, "Remember how we played this game. Today, on your turn, I want you to tell me something about the picture you choose. Let me show you. I'll say, 'I pick a card. I found a space shuttle. I wish I could ride on a space shuttle. Do you need the space shuttle?' Now, it's your turn. Remember to practice what kind of talking as we play?" Be sure to set up the game so the student wins and to model positive comments about losing such as, "Oh, I lost and you won. Oh well, I had fun anyway. It's fun to play even if you don't win."

Activity 4

Materials: any Memory Cards, Materials Book, pages 43 - 46

Homework: any Memory Cards, Materials Book, pages 43 - 46

Directions: Using word-initiation techniques, tell the student, "Remember how we played memory. Today, on your turn I want you to tell me about the pictures you choose. Let me show you. 'I pick a card. I got a zebra. A zebra lives in the zoo. I pick another card. I got a bed. I sleep on a bunk bed. They don't match. Your turn.' On your turn, remember to use bouncing, sliding, light contacts, and easy onsets."

Activity 5

Materials: any Track Board Game and matching Track Board Sentences, Materials Book, pages 70 - 79

Homework: any Track Board Game and matching Track Board Sentences, Materials Book, pages 70 - 79

Directions: Cut apart the sentences. Using word-initiation techniques, tell the student, "Remember how we played this game. Today, we'll practice bouncing, sliding, light contacts, and easy onsets as we make up sentences about the pictures on the sentence cards. I'll show you. I'll say, 'I pick a card. It says, "Here's a motorcycle." You should wear a helmet when you ride a motorcycle. I roll the dice. I can move two spaces. Your turn.' Be sure to use some bouncing, sliding, light contacts, and easy onsets when you make up your sentence."

If possible, arrange for the student to win and model positive comments about competition such as, "I had fun even though I didn't win. Maybe I'll win next time."

Activity 6

Materials: any Tic-Tac-Toe Category Cards and Tic-Tac-Toe Board, Materials Book, pages 122 - 126

Homework: any Tic-Tac-Toe Category Cards and Tic-Tac-Toe Board, Materials Book, pages 122 - 126

Directions: Copy the activity sheets. Cut apart the category cards. Cut out the Xs and Os. Place the category cards in a pile and place the tic-tac-toe board so you both can see it. Put the Xs and Os close by. Tell the student, "Today, we're going to practice bouncing, sliding, light contacts, and easy onsets while we name things in categories during a tic-tac-toe game. Here's what we'll say. 'I pick a card. It says, "Name three things you read." I read a book, a magazine, and a letter. I'll put an X here.' Your turn."

Periodically, ask the student to tell you why you're playing this game (e.g., to practice easy speech) and to tell you what she's to concentrate on (e.g., bouncing, sliding, light contacts, and easy onsets).

Activity 7

Materials: any Situation Pictures activity sheet, Materials Book, pages 114 - 115

Homework: any Situation Pictures activity sheet, Materials Book, pages 114 - 115

Directions: Cut the pictures apart and lay them out for a minute or two for the student to look at. Then, mix up the pictures and place them facedown in a pile. Tell the student, "Today, we're going to describe these pictures to each other to see if we can guess what's happening. We can only tell two things. Let me show you. I'll say, 'I pick a card. I see ____. They ____. Can you guess what's happening in my picture?'" Wait. "Good. Now it's your turn. Remember we're practicing easy speech so remember to include some bouncing, sliding, light contacts, and easy onsets."

Activity 8

Materials: What If...?, Materials Book, page 127

Homework: What If...?, Materials Book, page 127

Directions: Cut apart the pictures. Using word-initiation techniques, tell the student that in this activity you'll practice bouncing, sliding, light contacts, and easy onsets while reading and creating answers to "What if...?" questions. Place the pictures in a pile. Take turns asking each other the "What If" questions. Tell the student to answer in just one sentence. Remind her to use the target behaviors.

Activity 9

Materials: any Problem Solving, Materials Book, pages 128 - 131

Homework: any Problem Solving, Materials Book, pages 128 - 131

Directions: Show the student the Problem Solving activity sheet. Using word-initiation techniques, explain that you'll practice bouncing, sliding, light contacts, and easy onsets while reading about the problem and then figuring out the solution.

Say, "Today we're going to solve some problems. First, we'll read the problem on the top of this page. Before we start, though, let's look at the words on the page and pick ones for practicing our bouncing, sliding, light contacts, and easy onsets."

Have the student help select the words and underline them. Place letters over the words so you'll know which technique to use. "Let's read the problem together." Read in unison including the word-initiation techniques. "Now, let's take turns reading the clues and then telling what to do. I'll show you. 'The first clue says, "Tyrannosaurus Rex is in the middle." I'll write Tyrannosaurus Rex on the middle line. Your turn.' Read the clue and then tell me what you'll do. Remember to use bouncing, sliding, light contacts, and easy onsets in your reading and talking."

Activity 10

Materials: any Thinking Problems, Materials Book, pages 116 - 117

Homework: any Thinking Problems, Materials Book, pages 116 - 117

Directions: First, cut apart the pictures. Next, take turns reading the problem printed on each picture using word-initiation techniques. Then, mix up the problems and place them in a pile. Tell the student that you'll take turns asking each other how to solve the problem. Say, "This is how we'll practice bouncing, sliding, light contacts, and easy onsets today. Pick a picture and read me the problem. Then, ask me, 'What can I do?' I'll say, 'I can climb on a chair.' Then, I'll say, 'Your turn.' Be sure to use bouncing, sliding, light contacts, and easy onsets when you ask about and solve my problem just like I do on my turn."

Remember to reinforce the student for using the target behaviors by saying, "I liked the way you used (bouncing, sliding, a light contact, or an easy onset) on that turn."

Activity 11

Materials: any "What's Wrong?", Materials Book, pages 132 - 135

Homework: any "What's Wrong?", Materials Book, pages 132 - 135

Directions: Using word-initiation techniques, tell the student, "Today, we're going to practice bouncing, sliding, light contacts, and easy onsets while we tell each other what's wrong with this picture. Here's how we'll do it. We'll each look for something that is wrong. We'll take turns telling each other what's wrong. I'll start. 'I found something that is wrong.' You ask me, 'What did you find?' I'll answer, 'I found a horse with no tail. Your turn.'"

Periodically, ask the student to tell you why you're doing this activity and what the target behaviors are. Also, have the student self-evaluate by asking, "Did you remember to use (bouncing, sliding, light contacts, easy onsets)?"

Objective 6: The student will produce easy speech by using word-initiation techniques as cancellations, pull-outs, and preparatory sets in structured activities.

Procedure

In this objective, you'll teach the student that the word-initiation techniques can be used to cancel blocks, pull-out of blocks, or prepare ahead for difficult words or situations to prevent stuttering from occurring in conversation.

First, you'll practice the techniques in structured situations. In order to practice, the student needs to do some stuttering on purpose. Some students may find this difficult or unpleasant, but if you model the procedure first and explain the rationale, most students will be willing to attempt the tasks.

What if the student cancels at the end of the sentence instead of immediately? Tell the student that you liked the way she tried the difficult word again, but remind her that it's important to change the stuttering or hard talking immediately. Try some single word or phrase cancellations.

What if the student doesn't want to stutter on purpose? Model some stuttering and have the student imitate your stuttering. Then, model the stuttering and a cancellation or pull-out and have the student imitate you. By modeling you, the student may tune in to the characteristics of stuttering without the emotional overtones associated with her own stuttering.

What if the student really stutters when trying to stutter on purpose? Use this as an opportunity to discuss what the student does when she stutters. Let the student know that it's important to identify what hard talking or stuttering is like because then you can figure out what to do to change it to easy speech. Show the student how to use a bounce, slide, light contact, or easy onset to ease into the stuttered word.

Cancellations

Activity 1

Materials: Introducing Cancellations and Cancellation Practice 1 and 2, Materials Book, pages 147 - 149

Homework: Introducing Cancellations and Cancellation Practice 1 and 2, Materials Book, pages 147 - 149

Directions: Tell the student, "Today, we want to practice how we can use bouncing, sliding, light contacts, and easy onsets to help us cancel hard talking. First, let me explain what a cancellation is." Go over the Introducing Cancellations activity sheet. Model some cancellations. Then say, "Now I want you to practice some cancellations. I'll show you how." Use the Cancellation Practice 1 activity sheet. "First, I'll read this word. I'll pretend to stutter on the word and then I'll say it again using bouncing. Listen." Demonstrate. "Now, I want you to do the same thing on the second word. I want you to pretend to stutter on the word and then immediately say it again using one of our target behaviors. Which one do you want to use?"

If the student chooses a technique that won't work (e.g., a slide for a word beginning with a stop consonant), remind the student of the rules for using the target behaviors and have her select an appropriate one. "Good choice. Remember to change the word immediately before going on. That way you'll cancel the stuttering and replace it with easy speech." After you finish the words, do the sentences. Stop immediately after each stuttered word and cancel it.

61

Activity 2

Materials: any age-appropriate reading material, any Reading Practice activity sheet, or any activity that involves reading like Problem Solving, Materials Book, pages 128 - 131

Homework: any activity sheet used in therapy on which you've marked words on which to practice cancellations

Directions: Tell the student, "We can practice cancellations while reading. Let's go through this passage and underline some words we can pretend to stutter on." Underline at least one word in each sentence. "Now, let's decide which target behavior to use when we cancel the stuttering." Place a letter cue over each word. "Now, let's practice. We'll take turns reading a sentence and cancelling."

Activity 3

Materials: any Matching Pictures or Memory Cards, Materials Book, pages 31 - 46

Homework: any pictures used in the therapy session on which you have written directions for cancellations on the back

Directions: Cut the pictures apart and tell the student, "Today, we're going to practice cancellations while we describe these pictures. First, though, we have to decide which target behavior we'll use on each card." Go through the pictures and decide which target behavior would be good to use in cancelling stuttering for each word. Write it on the back of the card. Then, place the pictures in a pile and take turns selecting a picture. Tell the student, "I'll pick the first picture and make up a sentence about it. I'll pretend to stutter on the word and then I'll cancel the stuttering with a bounce because that's what we wrote on the back."

Then, have the student pick a card and do the same. To make this more fun, incorporate the naming activity into Picture Matching or Memory Card board games. If you do so, remember to let the student win. Model good sportsmanship attitudes.

Pull-outs

Activity 1

Materials: Introducing Pull-outs and Pull-out Practice, Materials Book, pages 150 - 151

Homework: Introducing Pull-outs and Pull-out Practice, Materials Book, pages 150 - 151

Directions: Tell the student, "Today, we're going to learn about pull-outs. Sometimes when we hard talk or stutter, we can catch ourselves before we finish the word and change to easy talking by using bouncing, sliding, a light contact, or an easy onset to pull-out of the hard talking." Go over the Introducing Pull-outs activity sheet. Then, say, "Now, let's practice pull-outs." Go over the Pull-out Practice activity sheet. Demonstrate how to start to stutter and then pull-out before finishing the word. Have the student practice pull-outs using the activity sheet.

62

Activity 2

Materials: any age-appropriate reading material, any Reading Practice activity sheet, any activity sheet with reading like Problem Solving, Materials Book, pages 47 - 55 or 128 - 131

Homework: any reading material used in therapy on which you've marked words on which to practice pull-outs

Directions: Tell the student, "We can practice pull-outs while we're reading. Let's go through this passage and pick out words we can pretend to stutter on and then pull-out of." Underline at least one word per sentence. "Now, let's decide how we'll pull out and put a letter cue above each underlined word." Have the student decide and write the letter. "Now, let's take turns reading the sentences. I'll go first. I'll start to stutter on the underlined word and then I'll use sliding to pull-out." Take turns.

Activity 3

Materials: any Matching Pictures or Memory Cards, Materials Book, pages 31 - 46

Homework: any pictures used in therapy on which you've written cues for pull-outs

Directions: Tell the student, "Now, we'll practice pull-outs as we describe these pictures. First, though, let's decide which target behavior we could use for each word and write it on the back of the card." Have the student decide and write the word or letter cue on the back. "Now, let's take turns picking a picture. I'll start. I'll pick a picture and make up a sentence. I'll pretend to stutter on the word and then pull-out using a slide because that's what we wrote on it." Take turns picking pictures and practicing pull-outs. To have more fun, incorporate this practice into a game format using the Picture Board or Memory Card games.

Preparatory Sets

Activity 1

Materials: Introducing Preparatory Sets and Preparatory Set Practice, Materials Book, pages 152 - 153

Homework: Introducing Preparatory Sets and Preparatory Set Practice, Materials Book, pages 152 - 153

Directions: Tell the student, "We can use bouncing, sliding, light contacts, and easy onsets to prepare ahead for difficult words and situations. When we remember to do that, we won't have to stutter. We'll just use easy speech." Go over the Introducing Preparatory Sets activity sheet. "We'll want to use a lot of preparatory sets in our next step (Transfer), but to get ready, let's practice some preparatory sets in some structured activities." Go over the Preparatory Set Practice activity sheet. Take turns using the target behaviors on the underlined words.

Activity 2

Materials: any age-appropriate reading material, any Reading Practice activity sheets, or any activity sheets with reading like Problem Solving, Materials Book, pages 47 - 55 or 128 - 131

63

Homework: any reading material used in therapy on which you've marked words on which to use the target behaviors

Directions: Tell the student, "Let's look at this passage. Let's pick some words that we might have trouble saying. Let's underline them and decide which target behavior we could use to talk easily instead of in a hard way." Underline selected words. "Now, we're prepared to use easy speech when we read. Let's take turns reading the sentences."

Activity 3

Materials: any Matching Pictures, Memory Cards, or Track Board games and matching Track Board Sentences, Materials Book, pages 31 - 46 or 70 - 79

Homework: any of the materials used in therapy which you've marked for preparatory sets

Directions: Show the student the game pieces. Tell the student, "Let's go through the pictures (or track board sentences) and pick some words we think we might have trouble saying. Let's choose a target behavior to use when we pick that card. We'll prepare ahead of time to use our easy speech." Have the student select some pictures and write a letter cue for the desired target behavior on each one. Tell the student, "Now, let's play the game. We can use bouncing, sliding, light contacts, and easy onsets while we play anytime, but we have to remember to use the target behavior on the words we prepared for."

Path 3

> **Goal 3.3:** The student will produce easy speech by using forward flowing speech and word-initiation techniques.

In this path to Step 3, model forward flowing speech as well as word-initiation techniques. Begin by introducing each technique separately. Once the student can produce each modification by itself, combine them. Follow techniques for introducing the modifications as described in Path 1 and Path 2. Then, alternate practicing the techniques in separate activities and finally, combining the techniques within activities.

Note: The path is set up to begin with forward flowing speech and then word-initiation techniques, but the order could be reversed if you feel the student needs to break up old word-initiation patterns before focusing on forward flowing speech.

As indicated in Paths 1 and 2, the incorporation of rate control and continuous phonation at all times addresses the motor component as does the focus on forward flowing speech.

Carefully controlling practice materials for length and complexity of linguistic content addresses the linguistic component. Some attempt has been made to incorporate semantically-appropriate tasks as well as to introduce pragmatic functions within the structured activity sheets and activities.

To address the psychosocial component, continue to use hierarchies to enhance the student's chances for success. Also, continue to provide a clear model and positive feedback to build the student's confidence in his speaking abilities. Encourage the student to participate in self-instructing and self-reinforcing and to take responsibility for selecting modifications, practice times, and outside support. Stress positive attitudes and self-advocacy.

For some students, once word-initiation techniques are learned, stuttering decreases significantly and the focus can be on forward flowing speech. For other students, however, use of word-initiation techniques are necessary as cancellations, pull-outs, and preparatory sets. Either way the goal should be on learning to produce speech in an easy way.

What if the student has trouble producing the modification? Encourage the student to produce it in unison with you at a very slow rate.

What if the student inserts a schwa into bouncing? Remind the student to produce the consonant and vowel of the word as a way of easing into the word. Don't allow the student to repeat only the consonant.

What if the student gets into a rhythm of bounces? Encourage the student to vary the number of bounces.

What if the student stops after each bounce? Remind the student that the sound has to keep going all the time. Show the student the differences using the examples on the Bouncing Rules activity sheet, Materials Book, page 137.

What if the student gets stuck on the consonant in a slide? Encourage the student to move forward into the following consonant or vowel. Demonstrate how to do this. Have the student focus on the feeling of the forward movement.

What if the student is tense during the techniques? Encourage the student to produce the techniques slowly and easily. Consider introducing some of the relaxation exercises, Materials Book, page 17.

What if the student has trouble initiating the easy onset or light contact? Remind the student to take the air in and then let it start back out before bringing the vocal folds or articulators together.

What if the student cancels at the end of the sentence instead of immediately? Tell the student that you liked the way he tried the difficult word again, but remind him that it's important to change the stuttering or hard talking immediately. Try some single word or phrase cancellations.

What if the student doesn't want to stutter on purpose? Model some stuttering and have the student imitate your stuttering. Then, model the stuttering and a cancellation or pull-out and have the student imitate you.

What if the student really stutters when trying to stutter on purpose? Use this as an opportunity to discuss what the student does when he stutters. Let the student know that it's important to identify what hard talking or stuttering is like because then you can figure out what to do to change it to easy speech. Show the student how to use a bounce, slide, light contact, or easy onset to ease into the stuttered word.

Attitudes/Advocacy

Stress attitudes such as:

- When I use forward flowing speech or a word-initiation modification, I am taking control. I am replacing old habits of hard talking with new habits of easy talking.
- I cannot stutter and speak easily at the same time, so I will choose to speak easily.

If you know an older student or an adult who has achieved success in controlling his speech through modifications, invite the person to join a session and talk to the student, demonstrating the use of the techniques.

Suggestions for Outside Support Providers

Home and School

Share Home and School Letters 3.1A, 3.2A, and 3.2B, pages 152 - 153 and 156 - 159, so the parents/significant others and teachers understand the techniques being taught. Also, share all of the activity sheets dealing with rules for use of the techniques. Invite the parents/significant others and teachers to join a session so the student can demonstrate how to modify his speech by using the techniques.

After the student has achieved success with activities in the session, send them home so the student can practice with his parents/significant others. Be sure to send directions so the support provider knows what to do and what to expect the student to do.

Ask the student's teacher if you can borrow a copy of the student's books so you can incorporate vocabulary and topics being covered in the classroom into the therapy activities. Once the student has completed some of the "What's Your Favorite...?" and "Ask Me" activities with the teacher in the session, assign the rest for practice in the classroom. Have the teacher and student select stress-free times for the practice (e.g., when it's quiet and no one else is around).

If you introduce Prolonged Speech, also send Home and School Letters 3.1B, pages 154 - 155.

> **Objective 1:** The student will be introduced to speech modifications of forward flowing speech, bouncing, sliding, light contacts and easy onsets.

Procedure

In this objective, introduce the student to five ways to modify speech production in order to produce easy speech. Use one therapy session to introduce each one, beginning with forward flowing speech and progressing in order through the other four techniques in the four subsequent sessions.

Activity 1

Materials: Introducing Forward Flowing Speech, Materials Book, page 18

Homework: Introducing Forward Flowing Speech, Materials Book, page 18

Directions: Tell the student, "We're going to learn an easy way to talk. It's called *forward flowing speech*. I want you to talk slowly and to run your sounds and words together like I do. Listen while I read these words, phrases, and sentences." Wait. "Now, I'll say them two times. Listen the first time and then say them with me the second time." Model a rate of 90-110 words per minute, using continuous phonation throughout. Later, you'll probably increase this rate slightly, but in the beginning the rate needs to be enough slower than the student's habitual rate so that he realizes there's a difference and so that he can concentrate on the feeling of moving forward in speech production.

Activity 2

Materials: Practicing Forward Flowing Speech, Materials Book, page 19

Homework: Practicing Forward Flowing Speech, Materials Book, page 19

Directions: Tell the student, "We're going to learn an easy way to talk. I want you to talk slowly and to run your sounds and words together like I do. Listen while I name and describe these pictures." Wait. "Now, I'll do these again two times. Listen the first time and then say them after me the second time." Model a rate of 90-110 words per minute, phonating continuously as you model forward flowing speech.

Activity 3

Materials: Introducing Word-initiation Techniques, Materials Book, page 136

Homework: Introducing Word-initiation Techniques, Materials Book, page 136

Directions: Tell the student that it's time to learn some other ways of easy speaking. These involve starting words in an easy way. Go over the activity sheet and define and demonstrate each technique. Review the Analysis Chart, Materials Book, page 13, on which you listed Bouncing, Sliding, Light Contacts, and Easy Onsets on the side with Easy Disfluencies. Tell the student that you'll start by learning bouncing. Next, you'll learn sliding and review bouncing. Then, you'll learn easy onsets and light contacts. After that you can practice all the ways to modify how you start (initiate) a word so that your speech will be easy and relaxed.

Bouncing

When introducing bouncing, describe the technique. Model how to bounce slowly with continuous phonation. Be sure to vary the number of bounces to insure the student is developing control. Discuss the value of bouncing (e.g., doing what you dislike) as well as its differences from repeating (e.g., it's slow, relaxed, and controlled). Also, remind the student that bouncing can be used on almost any word, making it a very useful technique. Encourage the student to describe the technique (e.g., "When I bounce, I repeat the beginning of the word in a slow easy way.").

Explain the differences between bouncing (a type of easy speech that involves easy disfluencies) and part-word repetitions (a type of hard speech or stuttering). Say, "You might think bouncing is the same as part-word repetition. In some ways it is. In bouncing we do repeat part of a word. It is different, though, because it is relaxed and effortless and we do it on purpose. At first, we will vary the number of bounces. Usually, we'll bounce one, two, or three times, but we could bounce 10 times if we wanted to. The important thing to remember is to bounce slowly and easily and to keep the sound going. We want to keep moving forward."

Sliding

When introducing sliding, describe the technique. Model how to slide in a slow, relaxed manner. Discuss the value of sliding and the words on which it may be helpful. Encourage the student to describe the technique (e.g., "When I slide, I stretch out the beginning sound of a word and ease into the next sound"). Be sure to have the student verbalize the sounds on which a slide *cannot* be used: stops and affricates.

Also, explain the difference between sliding and prolongations. Say, "Sliding might seem like a prolongation, but it's different. Prolongations are long and tense and we don't want to do them. Slides are easy and relaxed and we do them on purpose to ease us into a word. We'll vary the length of our slides, but we'll always make them move easily into the next sound."

Light Contacts and Easy Onsets

These can be introduced separately or together, but usually introducing them together is easier if time permits. Discuss how together these two techniques allow the student to modify any word. Encourage the student to describe the techniques (e.g., "When I use an easy onset, I bring my vocal folds together easily. When I use a light contact, I bring my speech helpers together easily.")

Activity 4

Materials: Bouncing Rules and Bouncing Practice 1 and 2, Materials Book, pages 137 - 139

Homework: Bouncing Rules and Bouncing Practice 1 and 2, Materials Book, pages 137 - 139

Directions: Tell the student that you're going to begin by learning bouncing. Go over the rules for bouncing and demonstrate how to bounce. Have the student say the practice words on the Bouncing Rules activity sheet with you in unison. Then, using bouncing, tell the student that you can practice bouncing in reading and in talking. Follow the directions on the Bouncing Practice activity sheets. Tell the student, "I'll read each word or sentence (or name or describe each picture) two times. I'll bounce on some of the words. Listen the first time. Then, repeat the sentence after me the second time. Be sure to bounce on the words just like I do."

Don't bounce on every word. If the student does well, repeat the activity sheets taking turns using bouncing.

Activity 5

Materials: Sliding Rules and Sliding Practice 1 and 2, Materials Book, pages 140 - 142

Homework: Sliding Rules and Sliding Practice 1 and 2, Materials Book, pages 140 - 142

Directions: Before introducing sliding, review the word-initiation technique of bouncing. Have the student practice bouncing in imitation using any activity from Objective 2. Then, tell the student, "Today, we're going to learn another way to use easy speech when we start words. Today we'll practice sliding. Remember how we learned what sliding was last time?" Go over the Sliding Rules activity sheet. Be sure to model sliding as you complete the activity sheet.

Then, go over the Sliding Practice activity sheets. Tell the student, "I'll read these words and sentences (or name and describe these pictures) two times using sliding. Listen the first time and then imitate me the second time. Be sure to use sliding just like I do."

Remember you can only slide on words that begin with vowels or continuant consonants. If the student does well, repeat the activity sheets taking turns using sliding.

Activity 6

Materials: Light Contact and Easy Onset Rules, Speech Articulators, and Light Contact and Easy Onset Practice 1 and 2, Materials Book, pages 143 - 146

Homework: Easy Onset and Light Contact Rules, Speech Articulators, and Easy Onset and Light Contact Practice 1 and 2, Materials Book, pages 143 - 146

Directions: Before beginning this session, review the word-initiation techniques of bouncing and sliding and practice them in any imitative activities from Objective 2. Then, tell the student, "We have two other word-initiation techniques to learn to use when we want to talk in easy speech. They are very similar. They are light contacts and easy onsets."

Use the Easy Onset and Light Contact Rules activity sheet and the Speech Articulators activity sheet to teach the techniques. Then, tell the student, "Now, we need to practice light contacts and easy onsets." Model light contacts and easy onsets as you complete the practice activity sheets. Say, "I'll read these words and sentences (or name and describe these pictures) two times. Listen the first time and then imitate me using light contacts or easy onsets the second time." If the student does well, repeat the activity sheets taking turns.

When you finish this session, tell the student, "Now, we're going to practice easy speech by using forward flowing speech and word-initiation techniques of bouncing, sliding, light contacts, and easy onsets in a lot of different activities and games." Move on to Objective 2.

69

Objective 2: The student will produce easy speech by imitating forward flowing speech and word-initiation techniques of bouncing, sliding, light contacts, and easy onsets in structured activities.

Procedure

In this objective, have the student imitate the different modifications. Initially, choose one type of target behavior to concentrate on in an activity, but as the student gains ability in using the techniques, combine them during the imitative activities. Remind the student that he should always concentrate on forward flowing speech by speaking slowly and easily. In addition, the student should use word-initiation techniques. Be sure you model the desired behaviors when giving directions and in conversation, not just during your presentation of the model to be imitated.

It isn't necessary to complete every activity in imitation. As soon as you feel confident that the student is producing the target behavior properly, move on to practicing them in activities which involve carrier/stereotyped sentences.

Activities: any imitative activities from Step 3, Path 1 or 2

Materials: appropriate materials for the activities selected

Homework: Follow the guidelines offered in Step 3, Path 1 or 2.

Directions: Follow the directions for the activities selected, adjusting the target behavior as desired.

Objective 3: The student will produce easy speech by using forward flowing speech and word-initiation techniques of bouncing, sliding, light contacts, and easy onsets in carrier and stereotyped responses in structured activities.

Procedure

In this objective, have the student practice the target behaviors in structured activities that involve carrier sentences (e.g., "I have a ____, I pick a ____, This is a ____.") and stereotyped sentences (e.g., "I pick a card. I put it here. It goes here. Your turn."). Model the target behaviors in your directions and conversation as well as during the activities. If you feel the words may be difficult or unfamiliar, go through them in imitation before beginning the activity.

Activities: any carrier/stereotyped activity from Objective 3 of Step 3, Path 1 or 2

Materials: materials as appropriate for the activities selected

Homework: Follow the guidelines for the activities selected.

Directions: Follow the directions for the activities selected, adjusting the target behavior as desired.

Objective 4: The student will produce easy speech by using forward flowing speech and word-initiation techniques of bouncing, sliding, light contacts, and easy onsets while asking and answering questions in structured activities.

Procedure

In this objective, help the student practice the target behaviors while asking and answering questions within structured activities. Model the target behaviors during your directions and conversation as well as during the activities.

Activities: any activities involving questions and answers from Objective 4 in Step 3, Path 1 or 2

Materials: appropriate materials for the activities selected

Homework: Follow the guidelines as described for the activities selected.

Directions: Follow the directions for the activities selected adjusting the target behavior as desired.

Objective 5: The student will produce easy speech by using forward flowing speech and word-initiation techniques of bouncing, sliding, light contacts, and easy onsets while formulating one or two sentences in structured activities.

Procedure

Help the student practice the target behaviors while formulating one or two sentences within structured tasks. Model the target behaviors during directions and conversation as well as during the activities. Be sure the student only formulates one or two sentences. The student will practice conversation under transfer.

Activities: any formulative activities from Objective 5 in Step 3, Path 1 or 2

Materials: materials appropriate for the activities selected

Homework: Follow the guidelines for the activities selected.

Directions: Follow the directions as given for the activities selected, but adjust the target behaviors as desired.

Objective 6: The student will use word-initiation techniques of bouncing, sliding, light contacts, and easy onsets to cancel and pull-out of stuttering moments.

Procedure

In this objective, teach the student that the word-initiation techniques can be used to cancel blocks and pull-out of stuttering moments. Let the student know that you'll practice in structured activities before trying do use these techniques in conversation. Take one day to introduce and practice cancellations. Then, review cancellations and introduce pull-outs. Take more time to introduce the techniques if needed.

In order to practice the techniques in structured situations, have the student do some stuttering on purpose. Some students may find this difficult or unpleasant, but if you model the procedure first and explain that it's important to learn what you do when you stutter in order to know how to change it, most students will be willing to attempt the tasks. Stress how the stuttering sounds and feels and contrast that with how the techniques sound and feel. Also, discuss how others might react to stuttering and how they might react to the techniques.

Activity 1

Materials: Introducing Cancellations and Cancellation Practice 1 or 2, Materials Book, pages 147 - 149

Homework: Introducing Cancellations and Cancellation Practice 1 or 2, Materials Book, pages 147 - 149

Directions: Tell the student, "Today, we want to practice how we can use bouncing, sliding, light contacts, and easy onsets to help us cancel hard talking. First, let me explain what a *cancellation* is." Go over the Introducing Cancellations activity sheet. Model some cancellations. Then say, "Now I want you to practice some cancellations. I'll show you how."

Use one of the Cancellation Practice activity sheets. "First, I'll say this word. I'll stutter and then cancel it using a bounce." Stutter on *sheep* and cancel with a bounce, "she-she-sheep." Have the student imitate you and then move on to sentences. Follow the directions on the activity sheet.

If the student selects a target that isn't appropriate (for example wanting to slide on a stop consonant), remind the student of the rules and guide the student in selecting an appropriate target behavior. Remind the student, "Remember to change the word immediately before going on. That way you'll cancel the stuttering and replace it with easy speech."

Activity 2

Materials: any age-appropriate reading material, Reading Practice activity sheet, or activity with reading like Problem Solving, Materials Book, pages 47 - 55 or 128 - 131

Homework: any activity sheet used in therapy on which you've marked words on which to practice cancellations

Directions: Tell the student, "We can practice cancellation while reading. Let's go through this passage and underline some words we can pretend to stutter on." Underline at least one word in each sentence. "Now, let's decide which target behavior we'll use when we cancel the stuttering." Place a letter cue over the word. "Now, let's practice. We'll take turns reading a sentence and cancelling."

Activity 3

Materials: any Matching Pictures or Memory Cards, Materials Book, pages 31 - 46

Homework: any pictures used in the therapy session on which you've written directions for cancellations on the back

Directions: Cut the pictures apart. Tell the student, "Today, we're going to practice cancellations while we describe these pictures. First, though, let's decide which target behavior we'll use for each one and write it on the back." Go through the pictures and decide which target behavior to use in cancelling stuttering on each word.

Place the pictures in a pile and take turns selecting a picture. Tell the student, "I'll pick the first picture and make up a sentence about it. I'll pretend to stutter on the word and then I'll cancel the stuttering with a bounce because that is what we wrote on the back." Then, have the student pick a card and do the same. To make this more fun, incorporate the naming activity into a Picture Matching board game or Memory Card game, but make sure the student wins.

Activity 4

Materials: Introducing Pull-outs and Pull-out Practice, Materials Book, pages 150 - 151

Homework: Introducing Pull-outs and Pull-out Practice, Materials Book, pages 150 - 151

Directions: Tell the student, "Today, we're going to learn about pull-outs. Sometimes when we hard talk or stutter, we can catch ourselves before we finish the word and change to easy talking by using bouncing, sliding, a light contact, or an easy onset to pull-out of the hard talking." Go over the Introducing Pull-outs activity sheet. Then, say, "Now, let's practice pull-outs." Go over the Pull-out Practice activity sheet. Demonstrate how to start to stutter and then pull-out before finishing the word. Have the student practice doing this using the activity sheet.

Activity 5

Materials: any age-appropriate reading material, Reading Practice activity sheet, or activity sheet with reading like Problem Solving, Materials Book, pages 47 - 55 or 128 - 131

Homework: any reading material used in therapy on which you've marked words on which to practice pull-outs

Directions: Tell the student, "We can practice pull-outs while we're reading. Let's go through this passage and pick out words we can pretend to stutter on and then pull-out of." Underline at least one word per sentence. "Now, let's decide how we'll pull out and put a letter cue above the word." Have the student decide and write the letter. "Now, let's take turns reading the sentences. I'll go first. I'll start to stutter on the underlined word and then I'll use sliding to pull-out." Take turns.

Activity 6

Materials: any Matching Pictures or Memory Cards, Materials Book, pages 31 - 46

Homework: any pictures used in therapy on which you've written cues for pull-outs

Directions: Tell the student, "Now, we'll practice pull-outs as we describe these pictures. First, let's decide which target behavior to use for each word and write it on the back." Have the student decide and write the word or letter cue on the back. "Now, let's take turns picking a picture. I'll start. I'll pick a picture and make up a sentence. I'll pretend to stutter on the word and then pull-out using a slide because that's what we wrote on it." Take turns picking pictures and practicing pull-outs. To have more fun, incorporate this practice into a game format using the Matching Picture games or Memory Card game, but make sure the student wins.

> **Objective 7:** The student will produce easy speech in structured activities by using forward flowing speech and word-initiation techniques of bouncing, sliding, light contacts, and easy onsets as preparatory sets.

Procedure

In this objective, introduce the student to the concept of preparatory set and encourage the student to use forward flowing speech, bouncing, sliding, easy onsets, and light contacts to help him prepare for difficult words or sentences. Do this in structured activities so the student will build up the habit of preparing ahead. This will then lead into the use of the techniques as needed in the transfer tasks which follow in Step 5.

Activity 1

Materials: Introducing Preparatory Sets and Preparatory Set Practice, Materials Book, pages 152 - 153

Homework: Introducing Preparatory Sets and Preparatory Set Practice, Materials Book, pages 152 - 153

Directions: Tell the student, "We can use forward flowing speech, bouncing, sliding, light contacts, and easy onsets to prepare ahead for difficult words and situations. When we remember to do that, we won't stutter. We'll just use easy speech." Go over the Introducing Preparatory Sets activity sheet. "We'll want to use a lot of preparatory sets in our next step (Transfer), but to get ready, let's practice some preparatory sets in some structured activities." Go over the Preparatory Set Practice activity sheet. Take turns using the target behaviors on the underlined words.

Activity 2

Materials: any age-appropriate reading material, Reading Practice activity sheets, or activity sheets with reading like Problem Solving, Materials Book, pages 47 - 55 or 128 - 131

Homework: any reading material used in therapy on which you've marked words on which to use the target behaviors

Directions: Tell the student, "Let's look at this passage. Let's pick some words that we might have trouble saying. Let's underline them and decide what word-initiation technique we could use to say them easily instead of in a hard way." Underline selected words. "We could decide to say the whole sentence in forward flowing speech, too. If so, let's underline the whole sentence. Now, we're prepared to use easy speech when we read. Let's take turns reading the sentences."

Activity 3

Materials: any Matching Pictures and Memory Cards or Track Board Games and matching Track Board Sentences, Materials Book, pages 31 - 46 or 70 - 79

Homework: any of the materials used in therapy which you have marked for preparatory sets

Directions: Show the student the game pieces. Tell the student, "Let's go through the pictures (or track board sentences) and pick some words or sentences we think we might have trouble saying. Let's choose a target behavior to use when we pick that card. We will prepare ahead of time to use our easy speech."

Have the student select some pictures (or words) and write a letter cue for the desired target behavior on them. Tell the student, "Now, let's play the game. We can use bouncing, sliding, light contacts, and easy onsets while we play anytime, but we have to remember to use the target behavior on the words and sentences we prepared for." Be sure the student wins.

Step 4: Desensitizing to Fluency Disrupters

> **Goal:** The student will modify speech production in structured tasks in the presence of fluency disrupters.

During this step, continue to model easy speech in structured tasks while gradually introducing fluency disrupters. Fluency disrupters include people, noise, movements, interruptions, varied locations, contradictions, time pressures, emotional topics, and competition. The student is expected to ignore these disrupters while continuing to use easy speech. In this way, the student learns to tolerate disrupters.

Using activities incorporated into earlier sessions, begin by having the student model your easy speech. Then, introduce a disrupter and continue until signs of impending disfluency are noted or it is obvious that the disrupter has no effect on the student's fluency.

You need not use a disrupter throughout a session as an intermittent disrupter is often more realistic than a constant one. For example, you might start and stop the disrupter two or three times within an activity. Intermittent usage will also increase the student's tolerance to interruptions.

At first, introduce only one disrupter (e.g., noise or other people). Work up to two to four disrupters per session. Instead of using the same disrupter in every activity, vary the disrupters within a session. Wait to use several disrupters at a time until the student has tolerated each disrupter separately. Use of combined disrupters (more than one per activity) is the last objective introduced.

If disfluency occurs, remove the disrupter. While stopping the disrupter may result in increased fluency, it may be necessary to re-establish fluency with choral reading, singing, rote responses, or rhymes and jingles. Reintroduce the disrupter after fluency has been re-established.

Objectives for this step are presented progressively in the order found to be most successful. It is important, however, to introduce them in the order that seems most appropriate for each student. Base your decision on your clinical observations and reports from outside support people. As you and the student progress through the activities, be sure to ask the student to tell you her target behaviors.

Home activities are not recommended in all areas of desensitization. Assign activities only when the student and outside support person are ready to handle them.

Suggestions for Support Providers

Home and School

Send Home Letter 4 and School Letter 4, pages 160 - 161, with the student. Descriptions of the disrupters used in therapy are included. The letters also state that you'll be contacting the parents/teachers in the near future because of the need to practice situations which they feel are disruptive in the home and in school.

Since many activities may be used to elicit several response types (e.g., imitative, carrier), be sure to provide explicit directions for the response type to be used when you explain how to use the activity.

76

Accompany your directions with the reminder that it's okay if the student does not model a response type exactly.

> **Objective 1:** The student will modify speech in structured tasks in the presence of people.

Procedure

Invite visitors to attend and participate in the sessions to desensitize the student to different people. Be sure that adults observe at least one activity before participating. Other students or young children can participate without any initial observation.

Tell the student that she is making good progress and that it's time to learn to ignore things which may result in talking the "old" way. Talk about the various disrupters that you'll introduce.

Explain that the first disrupter will be people. Take out the information lists completed earlier by family members and school personnel of people with whom the student has contact (See Suggestions for Support Providers, Step 1, page 8). Ask the student if the lists are complete. If not, have her add to the lists. Then, prioritize the people based on input from the student, reports from outside support people, and clinical observations. The list should include people with whom the student is acquainted and those who are strangers.

Invite those felt to be least disruptive to a session first. Progress to those people most likely to be disruptive. Initially, invite only one person at a time to a session. Later, invite small groups.

Inform visitors that you may invite them to leave at any time during the session if the student's fluency appears to be breaking down. You may even choose to invite a visitor only during the last activity. Then, if fluency disintegrates, you can complete the activity and thank the visitor for coming in a timely manner. Later, when the visitor comes for another visit and the student has maintained fluency, a longer visit may be appropriate.

Talk to parents/caregivers about introducing other people into home activities. If only one person has been doing home activities with the student, suggest that another child or adult be invited to join in some of the activities. Be sure that caregivers understand that this increases the difficulty of the task and that they should eliminate other disrupters by doing the activities in a quiet setting.

What if a visitor doesn't stay on task and instead, engages in too much conversational speech? Sometimes visitors forget the directions given at the onset of the session. When this occurs, you might say, "Guess what, (student's name). We forgot to tell (Grandma) that we try not to talk a lot during the activities. We wait until we're done."

What if a visitor doesn't use easy speech? Ignore it unless the student seems upset. If it appears upsetting, you might say, "Use easy speech, (Mr. James), just as we do." Later, remind the visitor about the need to use easy speech. Sometimes it's helpful to audiotape the visitors so that they become more aware of how their speech differs from the model.

77

What if the student begins to stutter during the time a visitor is present? Choose one of three options:

1. Finish the activity while continuing to model easy speech. Then, ask the visitor to leave by saying. "That was fun, but (Grandma) has to leave now. We'll practice a little longer and then we'll join her. Maybe she can come another day." After the visitor is gone, re-establish fluency. If the student has learned cancellations and pull-outs, discuss how they might have been used.

2. Stop the task temporarily and begin using unison responses. Say, "(student's name), we forgot to show (name of visitor) how we use easy speech in unison responses. Let's do it now. Let's count to 10 together."

3. Stop the activity and just tell the student to say some unison responses like reading sentences or reciting. Say, "(student's name), let's say these sentences together."

Attitudes/Advocacy

Tell the student that she can use easy speech even when there are a lot of distractions.

Cut out, mount, and send home the attitudes listed below and on page 154 of the Materials Book. Remind the student that she can use easy speech with everyone. Emphasize that she must not let other people bother her. Even if other people don't use easy speech, she should use the kind of speech that is best for her. Review attitudes which you have shared with the student and go over those you'll share during this step. Talk about where the student will put them so she'll see them frequently.

- I can ignore disrupters like noise and interruptions.
- I can do more than one thing at a time, like walking and talking in easy speech.
- I will set the pace for the conversation. My pace — easy speech!
- I can slow down a conversation by pausing and using my new way of talking.
- I can ignore pressure to speak quickly.

Suggestions for Support Providers

Home

If a family member or support person has observed and participated in therapy sessions and the student displays no significant increase in disfluencies, suggest that different family members or support people participate in the activities in the home.

School

Once the student has been fluent with a teacher in a therapy session, arrange some structured activities involving short responses which involve the whole classroom. Arrange a meeting with both the student and the teacher to discuss possibilities.

Activities

Materials: any appropriate materials from the activities in Step 3

Homework: appropriate pages from Step 3 in the Materials Book

Directions: Say, "You're good at using easy speech in the activities we've been practicing." Show Steps to Easy Speech activity sheet, Materials Book, page 10. "What are your target behaviors?" Wait. "Now, it's time for things to happen which might cause you to forget to use your new way of talking and go back to your old way. These are called *disrupters*. You have to learn to ignore them."

"We're going to repeat activities you've already completed successfully, but now we're going to make them harder by adding disrupters. We're going to 'toughen' you up or desensitize you to these disrupters." Show the activity sheet again. "Let's go over the disrupters."

"We'll start with people. We'll invite people to our session to watch and then participate." Take out the information lists completed earlier by family members and school personnel of people with whom the student has contact. "Let's make a list of all the people we could invite." Compile a list made up of people who are strangers and those with whom the student has contact. "Is the list complete?" If not, add more names. "Now, let's decide who would be least disruptive if they visited." Complete the list with the people perceived to be most disruptive at the bottom of the list. "In the beginning we'll only invite one person at a time. Later, we may ask a few people to come together. We'll start with (name of person perceived to be least disruptive.)"

When the visitor comes into the room, tell the visitor that you and the student will be using easy speech. Describe it. Suggest that the visitor use easy speech, too. After a few visitors have been involved in sessions, have the student tell the visitor what she is practicing. Then, follow the directions for any of the activities with the visitor present. Adjust the response level to include carrier/stereotyped responses, questions and answers, or short formulative responses as appropriate.

After the student maintains fluency with one visitor, add groups of visitors.

Objective 2: The student will modify speech in structured tasks in the presence of noise.

Procedure

To desensitize the student to noise, add competing noise while completing activities in this section. As nonverbal noise is usually less distracting than verbal noise, introduce nonverbal noise first. Be sure the noise is intermittent and not continued throughout a session. Use more than one kind of noise within activities and in subsequent sessions. While some of the noises you introduce may be regular in beat, make a conscious effort to make some of them irregular. Choose from any of the noises listed on the next page or add others.

- playing audiotapes or records which involve music, not talking
- moving or dropping pencils or paper clips
- ticking of a minute timer
- typing in the background
- tapping of a pencil or a finger on a table

After the student has achieved fluency with nonverbal noise, change to verbal noise. Choose from any of the following or add others:

playing unfamiliar vocal songs on a radio or audiotape. If fluency is maintained, play songs familiar to the student.

playing an audiotape which contains information usually interesting only to adults. If fluency is maintained, introduce an audiotape of interest to the student.

turn on a TV show of little interest to the student. If fluency is maintained, turn to a program of interest to the student.

Tell the student that you're going to introduce another disrupter — noise. Suggest that the student ignore it and continue using easy speech. When first introducing noise, tell the student the type of noise you'll be introducing prior to beginning the task. Later, introduce the noise without forewarning the student.

What if the student begins to stutter in the presence of noise? Phase out the noise and re-establish easy speech. Then, when you reintroduce the noise, have the student model imitative responses before increasing response difficulty. If the student has learned cancellations and pull-outs, model how they could be used and encourage the student to use them as you begin again.

What if the student doesn't stutter but appears upset by the noise or asks you to stop? Tell the student that you're going to continue the noise for a little while longer. Then, continue the noise for a few seconds and stop. Later, reintroduce the noise.

What if the student doesn't appear bothered by noise? Is it necessary to do all of the activities? No. Complete only as many as you feel are necessary. It is important, however, to introduce a number of different noises as you desensitize the student to noise.

Attitudes/Advocacy

Stress that the student can "tune-out" noise. Discuss the importance of being "toughened up." Compare ignoring noise to ball players ignoring fans or actors and actresses ignoring audience noises. Review the attitudes.

Suggestions for Support Providers

Home

Talk to parents/caregivers about introducing noise into home activities. If activities have been completed in quiet settings, suggest that they occasionally leave on a television or a radio. Have the parent or support person talk to the student about why noise is being introduced into the session. Also be sure that caregivers understand that the introduction of noise increases the difficulty of the task. Therefore, they should begin with very easy tasks. Also, ask them to eliminate the noise if the student begins to stutter.

School

No direct classroom assignments are recommended as noise is naturally present within a classroom.

Activities

Materials: any appropriate materials from activities in Step 3

Homework: appropriate pages from Step 3 in the Materials Book

Directions: Introduce the activity by saying, "Another disrupter is noise. While we're practicing easy speech, I'll start making some noise. I'll try to make you forget to use your target behaviors by making a lot of noise. What are your target behaviors?" Wait. "Don't let me make you forget. Ignore the noise. Don't let it bother you. This time, I'm going to make a finger tapping noise. Later, I'm going to make noise, but I'm not going to tell you about it. Let's start."

Follow the directions for one of the activities and add nonverbal noise. If the student is successful with the presence of nonverbal noise, add verbal noise to one activity in the next session. Once both nonverbal and verbal noise have been introduced, you may want to introduce nonverbal and verbal noise within the same activity (not simultaneously). Although you should not do more than one activity with noise within a session, be sure to use a variety of noises and make a conscious effort to make some of the noises irregular.

At the onset of each session, and if necessary at other times during the session, ask the student to review the behaviors involved with easy speech. These behaviors will be different depending on the modifications the student is using. Adjust the response level to include carrier/stereotyped responses, questions and answers, or short formulative responses as appropriate.

> **Objective 3:** The student will modify speech in structured tasks in the presence of movement.

Procedure

To desensitize the student to movement, engage the student in a fine motor task while completing any of the activities within this section. It is not suggested nor is it recommended that all of the activities be introduced in each of the fine motor tasks listed below. Instead, choose only those activities and types of fine motor tasks you feel are necessary.

It's important to realize that the activities included require the student to add movement to activities in which movement is not inherent. Most activities involve imitative or formulative response types. (Many Step 2 tasks have movement inherent within the task, and therefore, are not included in this objective.)

Movements might include:

- bouncing, throwing, or dribbling a ball
- making card towers or setting up Dominoes®
- walking around the room while talking
- modeling clay or Play Doh®
- painting, cutting, pasting, or coloring
- putting puzzles together
- building with blocks, bricks, logs, or Legos®

Point out that so far the student has practiced easy speech while sitting down. Now movement will be added to some of the same activities which she has already completed.

What if the student begins to stutter in the presence of movement? Let the student continue the fine motor task, but stop expecting speech for a few minutes. Then, reintroduce speech in a unison or an imitation format. If the student has learned cancellations and pull-outs, model how they could be used and encourage the student to use them as you begin again.

What if it doesn't appear necessary to do all of the motor tasks? While you should introduce a variety of movement types, it isn't necessary to repeat them again and again.

Attitudes/Advocacy

Remind the student that she can do more than one thing at a time. Give examples such as a ball player running and throwing a ball or an actor walking and talking. Stress that she can make speech muscles do what she wants them to do just as she can make arm and leg muscles do what she wants them to do.

Suggestions for Support Providers

Home

Talk to caregivers about introducing movement into home activities. Encourage them to have the student color, paste, color, model clay, or put puzzles together while imitating a verbal response. Be sure that caregivers understand that this increases the difficulty of the task, so they should eliminate other disrupters by doing the activities within a quiet setting with no other people present.

School

No direct classroom assignments involving movement disrupters are recommended.

Imitative Tasks

Activity 1

Materials: any Matching Pictures or Memory Cards, Materials Book, pages 31 - 46

Homework: any Matching Pictures or Memory Cards, Materials Book, pages 31 - 46

Directions: Cut apart the pictures. To introduce movement, you might say, "So far we've just been sitting quietly and practicing. What are the target behaviors we've been practicing?" Wait. "Yes, and as a result, you use easy speech. Sometimes it's hard to remember to use easy speech when we're doing something else, so now we're going to practice easy speech while doing some other activities. We'll try things like dribbling a ball, building things, and putting puzzles together. We'll be imitating words and sentences or making up short sentences while we do this. Here are some movements we might add. What would you like to try first?" Show the student a list of possibilities and let her choose. "Okay, let's start."

Have the student imitate you as you name the pictures while engaging in a movement activity. Vary the movement activity so that the student isn't making card towers or dribbling a ball during all of the imitative activities.

Activity 2

Materials: any Unemotional Situation, Sequence, or Rebus Story, Materials Book, pages 56 - 69

Homework: any Unemotional Situation, Sequence, or Rebus Story, Materials Book, pages 56 - 69

Directions: Review the components involved with use of easy speech. Wait for a response. Tell the student that you're going to read some sentences and want her to repeat them after you while doing something else at the same time. Show the list of movements to the student and ask her to choose one to do while she repeats what you say. Read any of the stories sentence by sentence. Ask the student to repeat each sentence after you using easy speech.

Carrier Sentence Tasks

Activity

Materials: none

Homework: none

Directions: Tell the student that the two of you are going to walk and talk about what you see as you walk. Then, take turns describing what you see in carrier sentences (e.g., "I see a door. I see a poster. Here is a mirror. This is a step.").

Formulative Tasks

Activity 1

Materials: any Matching Pictures and Memory Cards, Materials Book, pages 31 - 46

Homework: any Matching Pictures and Memory Cards, Materials Book, pages 31 - 46

Directions: At the beginning of the activity, you may wish to ask the student to describe easy speech.

Cut apart the pictures. Put all of the pictures in front of you. Tell the student that the two of you will take turns making up a sentence with two picture words in it. At the same time, the student will be doing something else, too.

Ask the student to choose the movement activity. After the student has begun the movement activity, pick up two pictures from the table and make up a sentence using both picture words. Explain that some of the sentences will be funny. Then, tell the student it's her turn.

Pick up the student's pictures if the movement chosen (e.g., dribbling a basketball) prohibits the student from picking up pictures during her turn. Have the student change movements if you use a large group of pictures.

Activity 2

Materials: Thinking Problems or Problem Solving, Materials Book, pages 116 - 117 or 128 - 131

Homework: Thinking Problems or Problem Solving, Materials Book, pages 116 - 117 or 128 - 131

Directions: Tell the student that you're going to solve some problems while she does something else. Let the student choose the movement activity. Then, take turns solving the problems. Have the student vary the movement if you'll be doing a significant number of different problems.

Activity 3

Materials: none

Homework: none

Directions: Tell the student that the two of you are going to walk and talk about what you see as you walk. Then, take turns describing what you see. Begin with carrier sentences (e.g., "I see a tree.") and then add a formulative sentence (e.g., "I think the leaves on the tree are pretty.").

Objective 4: The student will produce easy speech in the presence of interruptions.

Procedure

Arrange for interruptions to occur during any of the activities found in this section. Do only as many activities as you feel are necessary to desensitize the student to interruptions. Introduce interruptions while the student is modeling easier responses before expecting the student to model more difficult response types. Arrange the interruptions in the following progression:

1. environmental interruptions (e.g., leave the door open)

2. contrived interruptions (e.g., drop pencils or books)

3. movement interruptions (e.g., look away from the student, move materials, get up and walk around the room, or wave your arms)

4. people interruptions (e.g., arrange for people to knock on the door and come in to talk)

5. verbal interruptions (e.g., interrupt the student while she is talking to you by asking questions or making comments)

What if the student begins to stutter in the presence of interruptions? Discontinue the interruptions and re-establish easy speech. Reduce the response complexity when interruptions are reintroduced at a later time. If the student has learned cancellations and pull-outs, model how they could be used and encourage the student to use them as you begin again.

What if it doesn't appear necessary to do all of the activities? Do only as many activities as you feel necessary to desensitize the student to interruptions. You should, however, introduce each type of interruption at least once.

Attitudes/Advocacy

Tell the student that she shouldn't let interruptions bother her. If interruptions are nonverbal, they should be ignored the same way noise disrupters are ignored. If interruptions are verbal, the student should pause and then continue using easy speech. Stress the need to make easy speech a habit so that it won't be necessary to think about it all of the time. Stress the need to practice, practice, and practice some more!

Suggestions for Support Providers

Home and School

Because interruptions occur naturally at home and at school, no direct practice on this objective is recommended.

Activities

Materials: any appropriate materials from the activities in Step 3

Homework: appropriate pages from Step 3 in the Materials Book

Directions: To introduce interruptions, you might say, "Sometimes if something or someone interrupts you when you're talking, you might forget to use your target behaviors and go back to your old way of talking. What are your target behaviors?" Wait. "Good. When you use them you talk using easy speech. I'm going to interrupt you when you talk. I might talk to you, make some noises, or have someone else interrupt us. Don't let it bother you. Just keep using your easy speech. I'll really try to upset you, but ignore me. It's like a game. See if you can keep me from 'bugging' you. Let's try it."

Now, follow the directions for any of the activities and add interruptions. Arrange the order of the interruptions in the order specified in the Procedure section.

85

Adjust the response level to include carrier/stereotyped responses, questions and answers, or short formulative responses as appropriate. Be sure to introduce easier response types before more difficult ones.

At the onset of each session, and if necessary at other times during the session, ask the student to review the behaviors involved with easy speech. These behaviors will be different depending on the modifications the student is using.

> **Objective 5:** The student will produce easy speech in a variety of locations.

Procedure

To desensitize the student to a change in location while maintaining fluency, conduct the sessions in different locations while completing any of the activities found in this section. Do only as many activities as you feel are necessary. Initially, have the student model easier response types before expecting the student to model those which are more difficult.

Take out the questionnaire completed by family members and school personnel which was completed shortly after the student began therapy. Use this information as a guide. Also, talk to the student about how to set up a hierarchy of locations with those first on the list which she feels would not impact negatively on fluency and those last on the list which she feels might be more troublesome. Often locations just outside of the therapy room or within the same building may prove less threatening than those outside the building.

If questionnaires were not completed, consider the following location changes:

- just outside of the therapy room
- a different room in the same building
- outside the building
- a different building like a library or restaurant at a quiet time
- a park at a quiet time

Avoid noisy or busy times as these provide combined disrupters.

IMPORTANT: If leaving the building, obtain a Permission Slip, Materials Book, page 155.

What if the student begins to stutter? Finish the activity as quickly as possible. Then, return to the therapy room and re-establish easy speech. Try a change in locations at a later time. If the student has learned cancellations and pull-outs, model how they could be used and encourage the student to use them as you begin again.

What if it doesn't seem necessary to do all the activities? Do only as many activities as you feel are necessary to desensitize the student to different locations. You should, however, introduce a number of different locations, not just those in the school setting.

86

Attitudes/Advocacy

Stress these points:

- If I can use easy speech in the therapy room, I can use it anywhere.
- Progress is made in small steps.
- Lots of practice is needed when learning new habits.

Suggestions for Support Providers

Home

Be sure to obtain written permission for leaving the therapy building if you have not already done so.

Suggest that parents/caregivers change where they have been completing activities. Talk about moving to different rooms in the house or doing the activity outside of the home. Be sure that caregivers understand that moving to a different location increases the difficulty of the task, so they should eliminate other disrupters by doing the activities within a quiet setting with no other people present.

School

No direct school activities are recommended.

Activities

Materials: any appropriate materials from the activities in Step 3

Homework: appropriate pages from Step 3 in the Materials Book

Directions: Introduce location changes by saying, "We need to practice easy speech outside our therapy room. We're going to practice using easy speech in other places while we do the same activities we have done here. Let's make a list of other places we might go and then decide where to go first."

Work with the student to develop a hierarchy of locations using the information obtained earlier from the student and outside support people. Then, follow the directions for any of the activities and add a change in location to the session.

At the onset of each session, and if necessary at other times during the session, ask the student to review the behaviors involved with easy speech. These behaviors will be different depending on the modifications the student is using.

Adjust the response level for each activity to include carrier/stereotyped responses, questions and answers, or short formulative responses as appropriate.

Objective 6: The student will produce easy speech during contradictions.

Procedure

To desensitize the student to the contradictions she'll be facing during everyday speaking activities, it's important to introduce situations in which the student must deal with contradictions. Because contradictions tend to be difficult for many children to handle, it is suggested that contradictions be introduced only two or three times in an activity.

Two types of contradictions should be introduced:

1. The student will contradict (or correct) you.

Make a mistake, such as incorrectly naming a picture or incorrectly solving a problem. Wait for the student to correct you. Acknowledge your mistake. Say, "Oh, you're right. I made a mistake. I guess I didn't look very well. That's okay." If the student does not correct you, wait a turn and say, "Oh look. I made a mistake. Oh well." This acknowledgement is helpful in building an attitude that says, "It's okay to make mistakes."

2. The student is contradicted.

To accomplish the second type of contradiction, disagree with the student. You might contradict the student when she names a picture or gives the solution to a problem. Wait for the student to defend herself. When she does (or even if she doesn't), acknowledge your mistake so she won't be confused.

What if the student begins to stutter in the presence of contradictions? Stop the contradictions. Re-establish easy speech and reintroduce contradictions at a later date.

What if it doesn't seem necessary to do all the activities? Do only as many as you feel are necessary. Because contradictions are difficult for many students, try at least two activities with each kind of contradiction to provide sufficient practice.

Attitudes/Advocacy

Stress that it's often difficult to contradict or disagree with other people. Often this is because we're upset or in a hurry. If we practice, however, maybe we won't be as upset when we're contradicted or have to contradict someone. Be sure to emphasize that making mistakes is normal. Everybody makes mistakes. We often learn from our mistakes.

Suggestions for Support Providers

Home and School

Because contradictions often occur at home and at school, no special activities to target this objective are necessary.

Activities

Materials: any appropriate materials from the activities in Step 3

Homework: appropriate pages from Step 3 in the Materials Book

Directions: Follow the directions for any of the activities and add contradictions to the session.

To introduce activities in which the student must contradict you, you might say, "Having to contradict or correct someone who makes a mistake is often hard. If you have to do this, you might forget to use your easy speech. What do you do when you use easy speech?" Wait. "Good. I'm going to make some mistakes so that you can practice contradictions using easy speech. I want you to catch me and tell me what I've done or said wrong. Sometimes I may argue with you a little, but don't let that bother you. Just keep explaining why I'm wrong. Be sure to keep using easy speech."

To introduce activities in which you contradict the student, you might say, "For most people, it's even harder to fight for your own beliefs. Now, I'm going to tell you that you've made some mistakes even when you haven't. You're going to have to convince me that you're right. Try not to get angry or upset when this happens. And also, remember to use your easy speech. Don't forget that I'm pretending to disagree to help you make using easy speech a strong habit."

At the onset of each session, and if necessary at other times during the session, ask the student to review the behaviors involved with easy speech. These behaviors will be different depending on the modifications the student is using.

Adjust the response level for each activity to include carrier/stereotyped responses, questions and answers, or short formulative responses as appropriate.

Objective 7: The student will produce easy speech in the presence of time pressures.

Procedure

To desensitize the student to time pressures found in everyday speaking, present various time pressures while completing activities. Introduce only as many activities as you feel are necessary to desensitize the student. Introduce four types of time pressures:

1. increasing your rate of speech to a moderate or fast speed

Talk to the student about the need to keep using easy speech even if somebody else is speaking rapidly. Tell the student that you're going to increase your rate of speech to a moderate or fast speed while she continues to maintain use of easy speech.

89

2. introducing verbal time pressures

Talk to the student about the need to use easy speech even if you're being told to hurry. When you tell the student to "hurry," she shouldn't hurry her speech even if you begin teasing her about using slow speech.

3. imposing time constraints

A timer or stopwatch and a group of pictures are needed for this activity. A noisy timer or stopwatch is better than a silent one as the noise makes the student aware of the time factor.

Tell the student that there are times when it's necessary to talk a little faster. This may happen, for example, when playing some kinds of games. Tell the student that even though rate, one of the components of easy speech, may be quicker, she shouldn't speak so rapidly that she starts to force speech. Remind the student to integrate the other components of easy speech into her speech while increasing rate. Then, tell the student that you're going to practice increasing rate a bit while maintaining fluency during a timed naming activity. Explain that there are two methods you'll use to maintain fluency.

> Method 1: The student names a certain number of pictures (time yourself earlier to be sure that the number is realistic) within a specified time limit (30 seconds, 15 seconds). Then, if the student is fluent, ask her to name them again, but to do it in less time. Be sure to give the student enough time in the beginning to insure success as the noise and movement of the timer are sufficient pressures.

> Method 2: The student names as many pictures as she can in a specified time limit (30 seconds, 15 seconds). If fluent, ask her to do it again, trying to name at least one more picture than the first time.

4. imposing conversational time pressures

Tell the student that sometimes people make us feel like we have to answer questions or make comments quickly. In this activity, ask the student questions, but explain that you want her to use a two-count delay before answering or use a slow start and then speed up.

Try to successfully complete at least two activities with each of the four types of time pressures before moving to the next objective. If the student finds them difficult, do more.

What if the student begins to stutter in the presence of time pressures? Remove the time pressures and re-establish easy speech. Talk about what happened. Ask the student to tell you her target behaviors.

In all activities except those involving timed responses, reintroduce the time pressure. If the student has difficulty with a timed response activity, follow the preceding steps. Then, tell the student, "Say the words with me. Use easy speech." Keep saying the words with the student until fluency has been maintained for awhile. Then, gradually fade out. If the student has learned cancellations and pull-outs, model how they could be used and encourage the student to use them as you begin again.

What if the student can't think of a word during a timed response activity? Tell the student to skip the words she can't think of or assist her with a sound cue or multiple-choice cue.

Attitudes/Advocacy

Tell the student that she can resist time pressures. She can set the pace of a conversation by pausing (using time delay) and by using easy speech.

Suggestions for Support Providers

Home and School

Because time pressures often occur at home and at school, no special activities are needed to meet this objective.

Rate Increase

Activities

Materials: any appropriate materials from activities in Step 3

Homework: none

Directions: Follow the directions for any of the activities as you increase your speech rate. Tell the student, "Sometimes when you're talking to other people, you feel like you have to hurry up. That causes many people to stutter. Sometimes you think you have to hurry up if the person talking to you is talking fast. I want you to use easy speech even if somebody talks fast. What is easy speech?" Wait. "Good. So far, I've used easy speech during our therapy sessions. Now, I'm going to start talking (or reading) faster. Just ignore my fast rate. You keep talking easily. Don't let my fast talk bother you."

Adjust the response level to include carrier/stereotyped responses, questions and answers, or short formulative responses as appropriate.

Verbal Time Pressure

Activities

Materials: any appropriate materials from activities in Step 3

Homework: none

Directions: Follow the directions for any of the activities and add verbal time pressures. Say, "Sometimes people tell us to hurry up. Don't hurry your speech! Ignore them. Keep using your easy speech. What are the target behaviors which result in easy speech?" Wait. "Great. I'm going to tell you to hurry up while you're talking to me, but don't pay any attention. Use your easy speech and ignore it. Even if I tease you by saying things like, 'What's wrong? Can't you talk fast?', don't listen. Just keep using easy speech."

Adjust the response level to include carrier/stereotyped responses, questions and answers, or short formulative responses as appropriate.

Time Constraints

Activity 1

Materials: any Matching Pictures or Memory Cards, Materials Book, pages 31 - 42 or 43 - 46; a timer

Homework: none

Directions: Cut apart the pictures. Have the student name the pictures alone or at the end of a carrier sentence in the presence of a time constraint by using one of the methods described below.

Say, "Sometimes there are time pressures in games and activities. I want you to talk under time pressures. Talk as fast as you can and still use easy speech. If you feel you're going to stutter, slow down and concentrate on your target behaviors (e.g., forward-flowing speech, bouncing, sliding, light contacts, and easy onsets). It's more important to talk easily than to beat the clock or win the game." Then, explain the methods.

> Method 1: Ask the student to name a certain number of pictures in a specified time limit (30 seconds, 15 seconds). Then, if the student is fluent, ask her to name them again in less time. Be sure to give the student enough time in the beginning to insure success as the noise and movement of the timer are sufficient pressures.

> Method 2: Ask the student to name as many pictures as she can in a specified time limit (30 seconds, 15 seconds). If the student is fluent, ask her to do it again. This time, tell the student to name at least one more picture than the first time.

Once the student obtains fluency using one method, introduce the other method on another day.

Activity 2

Materials: Word Guessing Cards, Materials Book, page 156

Homework: Word Guessing Cards, Materials Book, page 156

Directions: Say, "Let's practice easy speech in a game with time limits. I'll show you how. I want you to guess the five words on my card. I'll give you a clue and then you try to guess. You have 30 seconds to guess all five words. Then, it will be your turn. The opposite of *old* is ____." Wait. "No. A grandpa is old, but a baby is ____." Wait. "Yes." Continue giving clues until the student has guessed all the words or the time is up. Take turns.

Conversational Time Pressures

Activities

Materials: any of the question and answer activities in Step 3, Objective 4

Homework: none

Directions: You might say, "Sometimes people will ask you questions and you'll feel like you have to answer them right away. Don't put that time pressure on yourself. Instead, silently count to two and then answer using easy speech."

You might also tell the student that another way to resist conversational time pressures is to "start slowly" and then speed up. This way the student gains control and confidence.

Follow the directions for any of the question and answer activities and add conversational time pressure to the session.

Objective 8: The student will produce easy speech in the presence of emotional topics.

Procedure

During the structured activities presented in this section, model easy speech as you express your emotions and describe emotional situations for the student. Explain that this isn't always easy to do. Gradually lead the student into expressing her emotions in short simple statements. Have the student imitate statements prior to formulating.

What if the student stutters in the presence of emotional topics? Finish the activity as quickly as possible or change a formulative task into an imitative or unison task. Use Step 1 activities to restore fluency. Reintroduce emotional topics on another day. If the student has learned cancellations and pull-outs, model how they could be used and encourage the student to use them as you begin again.

What if it doesn't appear necessary to do all of the activities? Because emotional topics often trigger stuttering, it's important to complete several of the topics listed. In particular, complete the Emotion Cards and Emotional Pictures, Materials Book, pages 173 - 174 and 213, and work through at least two of each of the types of stories.

Attitudes/Advocacy

Emphasize that the student can control her speech even when excited, upset, or under emotional tension.

93

Suggestions for Support Providers

Home

If a parent or outside support person has observed a therapy session and participated in at least one of the tasks and no stuttering disfluencies have occurred, send home some Emotional Situation and Emotional Sequence Stories, Materials Book, pages 157 - 164, after the student has completed them successfully in therapy. Be sure to instruct the support person on how to handle any disfluencies that may occur. Also, be sure that the support person understands that it's more difficult for the student to maintain fluency when talking about emotional topics, so an attempt should be made to eliminate other disrupters by doing the activities within a quiet setting.

School

No school assignments are recommended.

Activity 1

Materials: any Emotional Situation Story, Materials Book, pages 157 - 160

Homework: any Emotional Situation Story, Materials Book, pages 157 - 160

Directions: Review the behaviors associated with easy speech. Then, say, "Sometimes it's hard to use easy speech when we're upset, tired, angry, or excited. Let's practice using easy speech while we talk about some emotional topics."

Select an Emotional Situation Story. As you and the student are looking at the picture, ask her to repeat words which represent objects and also feelings using easy speech. Then, after reading each sentence of the story say, "You say that." Ask questions related to the picture such as, "What is happening here?" Wait. "What caused this?" Wait. "What will happen next?" Wait. Keep responses short (1-2 sentences).

Activity 2

Materials: any Emotional Sequence Story, Materials Book, pages 161 - 164

Homework: any Emotional Sequence Story, Materials Book, pages 161 - 164

Directions: Cut apart the pictures. Show the student the Emotional Sequence Pictures one at a time. Read the sentence printed on the first picture. Then, say, "Now, you say that." Continue until the story has been read. Then, ask the student questions related to each picture such as, "What is happening here?" Wait. Show the next picture and repeat the question. Keep responses short and use target behaviors.

Activity 3

Materials: any Emotional Rebus Story, Materials Book, pages 165 - 172

Homework: any Emotional Rebus Story, Materials Book, pages 165 - 172

Directions: Show the student the Emotional Rebus Story. Read the first sentence. Then, say, "You say that." Continue until the story has been read. Then, ask the student questions related to the story such as, "What happened first?" Wait. Keep responses short and use target behaviors.

Activity 4

Materials: student pictures and your pictures of people (e.g., her family), objects (e.g., boat, trailer, car, house), and pets

Homework: none

Directions: Review target behaviors. Show the student one of your pictures. Describe it in a carrier sentence. Say, "I'm going to tell you something about each of my pictures. Here's my first one. 'I have a house.' Now, show me one of your pictures. Tell me, 'This is my mom.'" Take turns. Vary the carrier sentences you use for each picture.

Activity 5

Materials: student pictures and your pictures of exciting family events (e.g., a wedding, a vacation, or a birthday party)

Homework: none

Directions: Show the student one of your pictures. Describe it in a carrier sentence. Say, "I'm going to tell you one thing about each of my pictures. Here's my first one. 'This is my birthday. I had a cake.' Now it's your turn. Tell me one thing about your picture." Vary the carrier sentences you use for each picture.

Activity 6

Materials: Emotion Cards 1 or 2, Materials Book, pages 173 - 174

Homework: none

Directions: Two methods can be used to introduce easy speech practice with the Emotion Cards.

Method 1: Cut apart the pictures. Pick an Emotion Card. Express a statement about that emotion and then, ask the student to tell you about her feelings on the same topic. Say, "We're going to talk about emotions. I pick a square. It says 'happy.' I feel happy when I go to the park. What makes you happy?"

Method 2: On the same day or another day, alternate cards. Instead of both of you talking about the same emotion, each of you will choose different Emotion Cards.

Activity 7

Materials: none

Homework: none

Directions: Review target behaviors. Roll a ball or car to the student. Use short sentences to tell the student how you feel about certain things. Use different feeling words. Then, ask the student to tell about something that makes her feel that way. You might say, "I feel happy when I go to the zoo. When do you feel happy?"

Use the following emotion words in your sentences:

happy	sad
laugh	cry
angry	afraid
like	don't like
like to do	don't like to do

Note: It is possible that at this point or at some point during desensitizing to emotional topics that the student will express some feelings about stuttering. Should this happen, go to the Branching Activity in Step 5, page 128.

> **Objective 9:** The student will produce easy speech in the presence of competition.

Procedure

Tell the student that while no one likes to lose, we all do sometimes. Have the student use easy speech in the presence of verbal competition and also when she loses a game.

Begin to introduce competition by arranging the game to be a closer match than previously (i.e., come close to winning). Then, present verbal competition by saying, "I'm ahead. I only need one more. I'm going to win." Finally, win a game.

What if the student begins to stutter in the presence of competition? Eliminate the verbal competition. If the game has been set for you to win and it isn't possible to change the setup, increase your positive statements. Say, "Even if I do win today, you'll probably win next time," or "Don't forget, it's fun to play even if you don't win." Then, use Step 2 or 3 tasks to restore fluency. If the student has learned cancellations and pull-outs, model how they could be used and encourage the student to use them as you begin again.

Attitudes/Advocacy

Stress that it's fun to play even if you don't win. Provide positive phrases the student can say when she loses such as, "Good game. Congratulations," or "Maybe I can win the next time." Review how to make positive statements during a game even when the other person is verbally competitive such as, "Good move," or "You got me that time." If the student wants to use verbal competition, remind her to be polite and to use slow speech.

Suggestions for Support Providers

Home and School

No direct work on competition is recommended, but you should discuss the attitudes being taught in therapy with a parent or school personnel so they can be reinforced at home and at school.

Activity 1

Materials: any Matching Pictures, Memory Cards, or Track Board Games and Track Board Sentences, Materials Book, pages 31 - 46 or 70 - 79

Homework: any Matching Pictures, Memory Cards, or Track Board Games and Track Board Sentences, Materials Book, pages 31 - 46 or 70 - 79

Directions: Review the behaviors associated with easy speech. Then, say, "Nobody likes to lose, but we all lose sometimes. The important thing to remember is not to let losing bother you. Continue to use easy speech. Sometimes when you're losing or when people tease you about losing, you might get upset and forget to use easy speech. To help you remember to remain calm and continue to use easy speech, I'm going to introduce some more competition into our games. I'm going to try to make you forget to use easy speech. I'm going to tease you if you get behind or make a mistake. Just keep using easy speech. If you want to tease me, too, that's okay. Just remember to continue using easy speech. Also, remember to be a good sport. Sometimes, I may even win at a game. Don't let that upset you and don't forget to keep using easy speech."

Model positive statements such as, "Don't forget, it's fun to play even if you don't win," or "Even if I win today, you'll probably win next time."

Follow procedures for playing the game. Initially, arrange the game so the student will come close to losing. Later, introduce verbal competition (e.g., "I'm ahead. I only need one more. I'm going to win."). Finally, arrange the game so that the student loses. Always make sure, though, that the student wins more games than she loses.

Adjust the response level to include carrier/stereotyped responses, questions and answers, or short formulative responses as appropriate.

After the student has played a few games using easy speech successfully, consider starting a game without making specific comments about using easy speech or being a good sport to see if the student remembers to do so.

97

Activity 2

Materials: any commercially available games previously played, like Go Fish® or Memory®

Homework: none

Directions: If desired, review the behaviors associated with easy speech. Remind the student that none of us likes to lose when we play games, but we all lose sometimes. Tell the student to use easy speech when people make competitive comments and also when losing a game.

Tell the student that the two of you are going to play a game. You may make some comments and might even win. Remind the student to be a good sport. Follow the directions for playing the game. As you play, model positive statements.

Adjust the response level to include carrier/stereotyped responses, questions and answers, or short formulative responses as appropriate.

Initially, the student will come close to losing a game, then will play in the presence of verbal competition, and finally, will lose a game.

Objective 10: The student will produce easy speech in the presence of combined disrupters.

Procedure

Now that the student has maintained fluency during the presence of one disrupter, it's time to introduce two or more at the same time. Introduce tasks in an imitative format before progressing to carrier/stereotyped sentences, question and answer, and formulative formats. Suggestions of combined disrupters follow:

- Combine contradictions in a different location.
- Combine interruptions and a different location by conducting therapy in a location where interruptions will probably occur (e.g., a restaurant, classroom, playground, ball game, gym) or where you can arrange for interruptions to occur.
- Combine noise and a different location by having therapy in a noisy office or a noisy classroom.
- Combine competitive activities with a different location.
- Combine people and noise by introducing verbal or nonverbal noise to one task on a day when someone has joined the session. Explain the procedure to the visitor prior to the session so that he'll know how to respond.
- Combine people and a different location by inviting someone to join you at the park, a restaurant, or in the library.
- Combine people and contradictions by introducing contradictions in one task on a day when someone has joined the session. Be sure that you have explained what you'll be doing to that person so he'll know how to respond appropriately.

- Combine people and competition by adding verbal competition or allowing the visitor to win a game. Talk to the visitor ahead of time so that he can respond appropriately. Include two competitive tasks within the session and arrange for the student to win the second one.

What if the student stutters in the presence of combined disrupters? Eliminate one of the disrupters. If fluency isn't regained, return to an imitated or unison response. If the student has learned cancellations and pull-outs, model how they could be used and encourage the student to use them as you begin again.

Attitudes/Advocacy

Review the attitudes introduced earlier in any of the steps.

Suggestions for Support Providers

Home and School

Because combined disrupters are often present within the home and at school, no special combined disrupters activities are needed.

Activities

Materials: any appropriate materials from the activities in Step 3

Homework: appropriate materials from Step 3 in the Materials Book

Directions: Follow the directions for any of the activities and add two disrupters. Tell the student, "Remember when I told you how I was going to try to disturb you by adding disrupters to our sessions? I've introduced all kinds of them and you remembered to use your easy speech. What did you do?" Wait. "Right. Now, because you've used your easy speech so well, I'm going to put a few of them together. Don't let the disrupters bother you. Keep using your easy speech."

Adjust the response level to include carrier/stereotyped responses, questions and answers, or short formulative responses as appropriate. Be sure to introduce easier response types before those which are more difficult.

During the session, ask the student to review the behaviors involved with easy speech.

Step 5:   Transfer

> Goal: The student will produce easy speech in real-life situations.

The goal of this step is to transfer the use of easy speech from structured activities in the therapy room to spontaneous speech in real-life situations outside the therapy room. In this step, the student practices each task or role-plays each task with you. As the student gains success, invite others to join the sessions so the student can gain success with family, friends, teachers, and other adults. By the end of the step, engage in real-life experiences such as, making real phone calls, going on field trips to restaurants and stores, and speaking to other people throughout the school.

To help you plan activities that are meaningful for each individual student, collect information (if you have not already done so) from the home and school regarding people with whom the student has contact, places the student frequents, and activities in which the student might be expected to speak. You can create your own questionnaire or refer to the family, school, and student information lists in *The Fluency Companion* [1].

Introduce the activities from each objective in this step at the same time. For example, instead of doing all Objective 1 activities before introducing Objective 2, select one or two activities from each objective to work on at the same time. This enables the student to work on a variety of transfer tasks and makes for more interesting therapy sessions.

Early in Step 5, model easy speech for the student using whatever target behaviors are appropriate. For the student completing Path 1, use forward flowing speech. For the student completing Path 2, continue modeling bouncing, sliding, light contacts, and easy onsets as cancellations, pull-outs, and preparatory sets. For the student following Path 3, model all of the target behaviors. By using these speech modifications, you'll be addressing the motor component. (To review information on Paths 1, 2, and 3, see pages 19, 41 and 64.)

Activities in Step 5 are organized around the pragmatic functions of informing, controlling, ritualizing, expressing feelings, and imagining. Utterance lengths and amount of formulation gradually increase in this step, moving from structured to semi-structured to unstructured speaking tasks. In these ways, the linguistic component is also addressed.

To address the psychosocial component, hierarchies are used, progressing from easier to more difficult tasks and enhancing the likelihood of success. Desensitization continues, but in a less contrived manner. Interaction with people within the home, school, and community makes transfer to real-life possible.

Throughout Step 5, provide a model not only of the easy speech target behaviors and language form, content, and use, but also of positive attitudes. Encourage the student to take an active part in the therapeutic process by assisting in organizing hierarchies as well as by self-instructing and self-evaluating.

---

[1] Karin Johnson and Barbara Heinze. *The Fluency Companion.* East Moline, IL: LinguiSystems, Inc. 1994.

Early in Step 5, you should keep disrupters to a minimum as dealing with the advanced response type (i.e., conversation) will be difficult enough. As the student achieves success and gains confidence, introduce disrupters into the transfer tasks (e.g., increase your rate, add contradictions, misinterpret what the student says, ask for repetitions and clarifications, ask the student to speak louder, ask the student to speed up, etc.).

Initially, tell the student that you'll be adding disrupters before doing so. Later, tell the student you may add disrupters, but you won't give him any warning. Encourage the student to resist the disrupters. Once you begin the real-life activities (e.g., going on field trips, presenting speeches, taking polls), disrupters will be present naturally so introducing contrived disrupters won't be necessary.

During Objectives 1-4, the student plays himself during role-playing activities. Later, the student gains practice imagining by reversing roles and by completing the imagining activities in Objective 5. It's important for the student to take on other roles to experience different rates, loudness patterns, pitches, and qualities. In doing so, the student gains a sense of control over the ability to produce speech.

Attitudes/Advocacy

Continue to reinforce positive attitudes and encourage the student to be an advocate for himself. Reinforce the idea that the student can control speech production by using the techniques learned.

Stress attitudes such as:

- I know what is best for me — easy speech!
- I can make my speech muscles do what I want them to do. I am in control!
- I can do many things with my speech. I can talk loudly, softly, quickly, in a high pitch, and in a low pitch.
- I can use easy speech any time, any place, with anybody!
- If I anticipate trouble, I have options I can choose to help me.

Share Attitude Cards 5, Materials Book, page 175. Encourage the student to place the attitude cards in places where he can read them often (e.g., on the mirror or in his notebook).

If the student expresses concern about teasing or expresses negative attitudes about stuttering, talk openly about his feelings and discuss options for dealing with teasing and ways to replace negative attitudes with positive ones. If teasing is a major problem, talk with the family and school support people to work out an approach to deal with the problem.

Suggestions for Support Providers

Home and School

Share Home Letter 5 and School Letter 5, pages 162 - 163, so the home support providers and teacher understand what you'll be doing in therapy. Invite the parent(s) and teacher to join sessions regularly so that the student can practice the target behaviors in role-playing and real-life activities with them. Guide the student and support providers as they make plans for transfer assignments.

Ask the teacher to suggest some classroom activities that you can role-play. Incorporate classroom materials into activities whenever possible.

> **Objective 1**: The student will use easy speech while informing.

Procedure

During this objective, introduce a variety of activities in which the student can practice the target behaviors while informing. Activities include narrative, expository, and conversational discourse tasks. Model each activity for the student using the target behaviors. Then, have the student practice or role-play each activity with you using the target behaviors. After the student is successful, invite others to join the session so the student can practice with them.

Whenever possible, provide the student with an opportunity to engage in a real-life situation such as a school assignment, field trips into the community, or assigned transfer practices. (See Transfer Assignment 1 and Transfer Assignment 2, Materials Book, pages 180 - 181.)

Review the home and school information lists (Use lists from *The Fluency Companion* or create your own.) for ideas to make the transfer process fit the needs of each particular student. The information will help determine the kinds of activities in which your student participates that you can then emphasize in role-playing.

Model the tasks using the target behaviors as appropriate for the student (e.g., forward flowing speech, word-initiation techniques, or both) and then encourage the student to participate in the activities and use the target behaviors, too. For the student who has followed Path 1, encourage forward flowing speech. For students in Path 2 or 3, use word-initiation techniques or both word-initiation techniques and forward flowing speech as preparatory sets. If the latter students have difficulty, encourage them to use cancellations and pull-outs.

To assist in transfer, have the student practice some of the informing tasks at home. Involve the student in planning the home practice activities, times, places, and practice partners.

Tasks in this objective focus on the following types of informing:

- giving and getting directions
- explaining procedures
- describing people, objects, places, and events
- retelling stories
- giving reports
- narrating programs
- making announcements
- giving recounts and accounts
- asking for and giving clarification

- comparing and contrasting
- conversing
- taking a poll and summarizing the results
- interviewing

What if the student stutters during transfer tasks? You have several options:

1. Drop back to an easier response type, regain fluency, and then attempt the task again.

2. For the student who has learned cancellations and pull-outs, demonstrate how they could be used in the transfer task and then try the task or a similar one again.

3. For the student who has only learned forward flowing speech, if the difficulty seems to be related to word-initiation, consider introducing word-initiation techniques and then return to Step 3 and follow Path 3.

What if the student increases the rate of speech in the conversational tasks? If the student remains fluent, don't be concerned, but continue to model a slightly slower rate in your speech. Encourage the student to begin each utterance slowly.

What if the student doesn't seem aware of his disfluencies or doesn't try to pull-out or cancel stuttering moments? Try taping a session and playing back the moments. Discuss how to use the target behaviors to cancel or pull-out of a block. Practice on the stuttered words from the tape. Review how to prepare ahead to use easy speech.

What if the student uses easy speech with you, but forgets when others join the session? Prior to the session, talk about the need to use easy speech with others. Discuss ways to cue the student with hand gestures to remind him to use the target behaviors. To ease into the activities, do something simple with the visitor before trying the transfer tasks. Also, at the beginning of the session, tell the visitor what the student will be practicing and have the student demonstrate the target behaviors.

What if the student avoids words like his name or words beginning with certain sounds? Talk about the importance of approaching, not avoiding, difficult words. If the student knows word-initiation techniques, talk about how to prepare ahead to use one of the target behaviors. Remind the student to speak slowly and easily and to focus on moving forward, running the sounds and words together. If the student is on Path 1, simply put some of the techniques into your modeling without labeling them. If more direct work is needed, introduce the techniques from Path 2 as some other ways to use easy speech.

What if the student has trouble talking on the phone? Make the initial practice easier by having the student recite or read a familiar passage to you on the phone before actually having a conversation.

Activity 1

Materials: any Direction Pictures or Maps, Materials Book, pages 120 - 121 or 176 - 179 (or any map)

Homework: any Direction Pictures or Maps, Materials Book, pages 120 - 121 or 176 - 179

Directions: Show the student a Direction Picture or a map. Say, "Sometimes we have to give people directions or ask for directions. Today, we're going to practice using our target behaviors while we give directions to places. I'll go first. I'll use (name a target behavior) while I tell how to get to _____." Model the directions. Then, say, "Now, you pick a place. How do you get there? What target behavior(s) will you use while you tell me?"

Take turns asking for and giving directions to places on the Direction Pictures or Maps. When you're finished, talk about times when you might have had to give or get directions. Act out some of these situations (e.g., pretend you're a school visitor and ask the student for directions to the office; pretend you're a stranger at the mall and ask the student where the rest room is).

Activity 2

Materials: none

Homework: Transfer Assignment 1, completed for giving directions at home, Materials Book, page 180

Directions: Follow the directions for Activity 1, but name a location in the student's school or community. Have the student give you directions from the therapy room to that location.

Places

School	*Community*
rest room	student's home
water fountain	park
main entrance	donut shop
gym	ball field
main office	ice cream store
playground	hair salon/barbershop
kindergarten room	fast-food restaurant
library	library
cafeteria	gas station
principal's office	movie theater

When you're finished, talk about when you might have had to give directions. Role-play being someone and asking the student for directions.

Activity 3

Materials: Explanation Cards, Materials Book, page 182

Homework: Explanation Cards, Materials Book, page 182

Directions: Cut the cards apart. Show the student the Explanation Cards. Select a card and say, "Sometimes we have to explain how to do things. Today, we'll practice our target behavior(s) while explaining how to do some things. I'll show you. I'll use (target behavior) while I tell you how to bake cookies."

When you're finished say, "Now, you pick a card. How do you do that? Tell me how to do what it says. What will you practice while you tell me?"

Take turns asking for and giving explanations. Talk about when you might have to give explanations.

Activity 4

Materials: Tricks 1 or 2 and Experiments, Materials Book, pages 183 - 185

Homework: Tricks 1 or 2 and Experiments, Materials Book, pages 183 - 185

Directions: Tell or show the student how to complete any of the tricks or experiments on the activity sheets. Then, say, "Now, I want you to use your target behavior(s) while you explain to me how to (do a card trick). Pretend I don't know how."

After the student is successful on these tasks, invite others to your room and have the student tell them the procedure. After he is successful with others, consider having the student teach a group of students either in the therapy room or in the classroom. Have the student teach someone at home how to do the procedure.

Activity 5

Materials: any game, Materials Book, pages 70 - 102, or any other game or sport

Homework: Transfer Assignment 2, Materials Book, page 181

Directions: Tell the student, "Today, I want you to pretend I don't know how to play ____. I want you to practice your target behavior(s) while you tell me. What will you concentrate on?"

Activity 6

Materials: any object in the room or objects the student brings from home and Description Guide, Materials Book, page 186

Homework: Transfer Assignment 1 or 2 and Description Guide, completed for a describing assignment, Materials Book, page 180 or 181 and page 186

Directions: Tell the student, "Sometimes we have to describe things. I want you to practice your target behaviors while describing objects in our room. Tell me five or six different things. You can use the Description Guide to help you think of things to tell me. I'll show you how first. I'll describe my desk. I'll use (target behavior)."

105

Activity 7

Materials: any Family or Community Worker Puppets, Materials Book, pages 187 - 194

Homework: any Family or Community Worker Puppets, Materials Book, pages 187 - 194

Directions: Tell the student, "Sometimes we have to describe people. Let's pretend someone is at the door. I want to know who it is. You pick a picture of a person and describe that person to me. Remember to use your target behaviors while you're describing the person."

Activity 8

Materials: any Direction Pictures, Materials Book, pages 120 - 121

Homework: any Direction Pictures, Materials Book, pages 120 - 121

Directions: Tell the student, "Sometimes we have to describe places. Let's pretend I don't know where you are. Pick a location and describe it for me so I know where you are. Which target behavior will you use while you tell me?"

Activity 9

Materials: any Unemotional or Emotional Situation Story, Materials Book, pages 56 - 59 or 157 - 160

Homework: any Unemotional or Emotional Situation Story and Transfer Assignment 2, completed for describing, Materials Book, pages 56 - 59, 157 - 160 and page 181

Directions: Tell the student, "Sometimes we have to describe events. I want you to tell me about this picture. Don't tell me a story, just describe what you see. You can use this time to practice your target behavior(s)."

Activity 10

Materials: none

Homework: Transfer Assignment 1, completed for a description of an event, Materials Book, page 180

Directions: Tell the student, "Sometimes people ask us to tell about something we've seen or done. Let's take turns describing an event to each other. I'll go first. I'll use (target behavior) while I describe my vacation. Then, it'll be your turn. What do you want to describe? What will you practice?"

Encourage the student to suggest events of interest. Some suggestions are listed below. After completing the task, invite others to join the session and have the student describe an event or tell what you did in the session.

Events

school play	concert
birthday party	picnic
championship ball game	spelling bee
science fair	aquarium visit
amusement park	talent show

Activity 11

Materials: any Unemotional or Emotional Situation, Sequence, or Rebus Story, Materials Book, pages 56 - 69 or 157 - 172

Homework: any Unemotional or Emotional Situation, Sequence, or Rebus Story, Materials Book, pages 56 - 69 or 157 - 172

Directions: Tell the student, "Many times people ask us to tell a story. Telling a story is a good time to practice easy speech." Show the student one of the stories. "I want you to skim through this story that we read before. Then, I want you to retell the story to me. What target behaviors will you use?"

Activity 12

Materials: familiar books, movies, or television shows

Homework: Transfer Assignment 2, completed to retell a story, Materials Book, page 181

Directions: Tell the student, "Many times people ask us to tell them about a story from a book, movie, or television show. That's a good time to practice easy speech. I'll tell you about a show I saw last night. I'm going to use (target behavior). You think of a story to tell me when I'm done."

Activity 13

Materials: any Story Puppets, Materials Book, pages 195 - 198

Homework: any Story Puppets, Materials Book, pages 195 - 198

Directions: Set up the puppets. Tell the story in an abbreviated form. Model the target behaviors in your speech. Then, tell the student to retell the story using his target behaviors.

Activity 14

Materials: none

Homework: Transfer Assignment 2, Materials Book, page 181, completed for practicing a report with a support person

Directions: Tell the student, "Sometimes you have to give oral reports or speeches in class. Today, we're going to practice giving reports. I want you to stand and face me. Pretend I'm in your class. Then, give me a report on your favorite game. This is a good time to practice your easy speech."

In the beginning, assign topics. When the student is ready, let him choose a topic of his own. Talk with the teacher to see if there's an assignment you should practice in class.

At first, be a good listener for the student. Later, tell the student, "Sometimes it's hard to concentrate when giving a report. There might be sounds or movements that distract you. To help you learn to ignore the distractions, I'm going to do some things that might happen in your class during your speech. Don't let me bother you. Don't let me make you forget your easy speech." Then, while the student is giving his speech, cough, drop books, sneeze, tap a pencil, whisper, etc. Afterward, talk about whether these things bothered the student.

After the student has experienced success, invite another person or several others to join the session to listen to the report. If possible, go to an empty classroom and have the student present the report to you or to several people. If the student has to give a report in class, try to have the teacher attend a session in which the student practices the report. Ask the student if he would like you to attend class on the day of the report.

Activity 15

Materials: Programs, Materials Book, page 199; and a pretend or real microphone

Homework: Programs, Materials Book, page 199

Directions: Cut the activity sheet apart and tell the student, "Sometimes people are asked to narrate programs at school or other places. Narrators have to speak slowly and easily so people can understand them. Pretending to narrate a program is a good way to practice your easy speech." Give the student the activity sheet and say, "Here are some examples of programs you could narrate. Let's use easy speech while we talk about what you could say. Then, I want you to stand up and pretend to narrate the program. You can pretend you're using this microphone."

After the student is successful, invite others to the session and have the student practice for them. Then, go to a gym or auditorium and have the student stand on the stage and pretend to narrate a program.

Activity 16

Materials: Announcements, Materials Book, page 200; and a real or pretend microphone

Homework: Announcements, Materials Book, page 200

Directions: Tell the student, "Sometimes you have to make announcements at school. People who make announcements need to use easy speech so other people can understand. Let's practice making a school announcement. What target behaviors will you use?"

Start by having the student read the announcements on the activity sheet. If the student is using word-initiation modifications, you might have him prepare ahead by underlining words on which to use the techniques. Later, have the student create original announcements.

Have the student stand and pretend to make the announcements into a microphone. If you're in a facility with a P.A. system, get permission to have the student pretend to make the announcements over the P.A. system. Progress to making an announcement to your room. If possible, have the student make a real announcement over the P.A. system. Begin by making it to only one room, perhaps for a younger grade. Progress to making the announcement to his class or the entire school. Always practice in the therapy room and P.A. room before turning on the machine.

Activity 17

Materials: none

Homework: Transfer Assignment 1, Materials Book, page 180, completed for giving an account of the session to the outside support person

Directions: Near the end of any session, tell the student, "Sometimes we have to tell people about what we've done. Before you leave, I want you to tell me all about what we've done today. Use your target behaviors." Invite others to join the end of a session occasionally and have the student give an account of the session's activities.

Activity 18

Materials: none

Homework: none

Directions: At the beginning of any session, tell the student, "I want you to practice your target behaviors while you tell me (what you did in school today, what you did over the weekend, what you did last night, etc)."

Activity 19

Materials: none

Homework: none

Directions: Tell the student that sometimes you have to ask for or give clarification. Say, "Today, we're going to role-play some situations in which we need to ask for or give more information. We'll practice our target behaviors while we pretend. I want you to be you. I'll be the other person." Some suggested situations are listed on the next page.

109

Situations

- The student wants a library book he can't reach. The librarian asks which one.
- The student wants a new bike. The parent asks which one.
- The student wants a dessert in the cafeteria. A worker asks which one.
- The student wants to buy a concert ticket. The clerk asks which type.
- The teacher asks the student to get some books on the shelf. The student asks which ones.
- The coach asks the student to get some supplies. The student asks which ones.
- The principal asks the student to set up the gym. The student asks how.
- The student asks his parent how to set the table.
- The student asks his parent how to put up party decorations.
- The student asks his teacher how to head (put name and date on) his homework.
- The student asks his teacher how to arrange the bulletin board.
- The student asks his parent how to clean the pet cage.

Activity 20

Materials: Barrier Pictures, Materials Book, page 201; two blank sheets of paper; a barrier (e.g., a box or a folder)

Homework: Barrier Pictures, Materials Book, page 201; blank sheets of paper; a barrier

Directions: Make two copies of the barrier pictures and cut them apart. Place a blank sheet of paper in front of each of you and then place a barrier between you. Make sure each of you has a set of barrier pictures. Tell the student, "Sometimes we have to ask for or give information to help people understand what we want them to do. Today, we're going to play a barrier game. We'll practice easy speech while we tell each other where to put the pieces. If we don't understand the directions, we'll have to ask for more information. What will we practice while we play?" Wait. Tell the student, "I'll go first. Put the little tree in the corner." See if the student asks, "Which corner?" When you're finished, compare pictures and see how well they match.

Activity 21

Materials: Venn Diagram and Compare and Contrast Pictures 1 or 2, Materials Book, pages 202 - 204

Homework: Transfer Assignment 2, completed to compare and contrast something, Venn Diagram, and Compare and Contrast Pictures 1 or 2, Materials Book, pages 181 and 202 - 204

Directions: Cut apart the pictures. Tell the student, "Sometimes we have to compare and contrast two things. Today, we'll compare and contrast things to practice our easy speech." Show the completed Venn Diagram. Say, "Look at this diagram. It shows how a car and a truck are the same and different. I can look at this and use it to help me tell how they are the same and different. Listen."

Model a compare/contrast speech using the target behaviors. "Now, let's look at this blank diagram. Let's use it to get ideas for comparing and contrasting two things. Put out compare/contrast pictures. Select a compare/contrast picture and fill in a blank Venn Diagram for the objects shown."

While you complete the chart, talk with the student and model the target behaviors in your speech. Remind the student to use them as needed. When the chart is complete, tell the student, "Now, use the chart as a guide and tell me how these things are the same and different. Tell me the same things first and then the differences. What will you practice while you're talking?"

Encourage the student to look for similarities and differences in category, function, attributes, composition, etc. Encourage the student to use words like *and* and *both* for similarities and *not*, *doesn't*, and comparison (*-er*) for differences.

After the student is capable of doing compare/contrast tasks with the pictures, try just presenting ideas. Likewise, once the student gets the idea, stop using the Venn Diagram.

Compare and Contrast Tasks

Washington and Lincoln	Mayan and Incan Indians
football and baseball	Snow White and Cinderella
soccer and basketball	book and magazine
train and plane	pie and cake
pencil and crayon	camper and tent
glue and stapler	flower and tree
shoe and boot	doll and stuffed animal

Activity 22

Materials: none

Homework: none

Directions: Engage the student in conversation about topics of interest. Ask the student to choose from the suggested topics or pick his own topic. Say, "Today, let's just talk and practice our easy speech while we talk. Let's talk about . . ."

Topics

prehistoric animals	magazines	snacks
computer games	arcades	books
sports	tricks	collections
crafts	clubs/organizations	records/tapes/CDs
holidays	toys	vacations
allowances	chores	outer space

111

Activity 23

Materials: paper, a pencil, and poster board (optional)

Homework: none

Directions: Tell the student, "Sometimes we want to gather information from a lot of people. Then, we take a poll. After we get the information, we can summarize it. We can practice easy speech as we gather the information and again as we summarize the findings. Let's pretend we want to take a poll of the people in our building. Let's see which team they think will (win the Super Bowl). First, you'll introduce yourself and then you'll explain what we're doing. Be sure to thank the person when you're done. Pretend I'm the principal. Ask me for my opinion. Be sure to use easy speech."

Pretend to be other people in the building and have the student continue the poll. Tell the student that you might ask some unexpected questions. Remind the student to keep using easy speech.

After the student is successful, go around the building and take a real poll. Choose a topic from the list below. Tell the student you'll be close by, but he'll do all the talking. As you walk around, model easy speech for the student in your conversation. Talk to the student's teacher about letting the student take a poll in his classroom.

When you're finished, return to your room. Tell the student, "Now, let's keep practicing easy speech while we talk about the results." After you tally the results, ask the student to pretend to give a summary report to his class. You could even make a chart to use while giving the summary report. If possible, the student could give an actual summary report to his class.

Topics

winner of an election	best movie
best magazine	best sport
best holiday	best instrument
best vacation	best car
best TV show/channel	winner of a contest

Activity 24

Materials: Interview Questions, Materials Book, page 205

Homework: Interview Questions, Materials Book, page 205

Directions: Tell the student, "Sometimes we're asked to interview people. This is a good time to practice our target behaviors. Let's pretend by using this interview sheet. I'll interview you first and then you can interview me. Remember to use your target behaviors."

After the student has achieved success, arrange for the student to interview other people at home and at school. Role-play the interviews first.

Objective 2: The student will use easy speech while ritualizing.

Procedure

In this objective, the student practices easy speech in activities which focus on the pragmatic function of ritualizing. Have the student role-play rituals with you and then invite others to join the session so the student can practice more realistic situations. Continue to assign home practice. Involve the student in selecting activities and planning outside practice activities.

Model the tasks using the target behaviors as appropriate for the student (i.e., forward flowing speech, word-initiation techniques, or both) and then encourage the student to participate in the activities and use the target behaviors, too. For the student who has followed Path 1, encourage forward flowing speech. For students in Path 2 or 3, use word-initiation techniques or both word-initiation techniques and forward flowing speech as preparatory sets. If the latter students have difficulty, encourage them to use cancellations and pull-outs.

Activities in this objective target rituals associated with:

- introductions
- phone calls
- ordering in a restaurant
- getting someone's attention
- telling jokes
- greeting and departing phrases
- taking and giving messages
- taking orders and requesting donations
- making and accepting or rejecting invitations

Introductions

Activity 1

Materials: none

Homework: Transfer Assignment 1 or 2, Materials Book, page 108 or 181, completed for pretending introductions

Directions: Tell the student, "Sometimes we have to introduce people to each other. You may feel uncomfortable or pressured to speak quickly and forget to use easy speech so we need to practice. Pretend you need to introduce me to your teacher. You would say, 'Miss Jones, this is my teacher, Mr. Black. Mr. Black, this is my speech teacher, Miss Jones.' Now, you try."

Be sure to model the target behaviors on your turn and remind the student to use them as needed. Ask the student to help you make a list of people to practice introducing you to. Some ideas are listed below. Have the student select the order for practicing the introductions.

parents	grandparents
coach	music teacher
teacher	friend
cousin	baby-sitter
aunt/uncle	sibling
principal	school nurse
secretary	P.E. teacher
cafeteria worker	custodian

After the student is successful in role-playing, invite people to the session and practice introductions. Later, go around the building and practice introductions with people in the building. If possible, tell the people in advance that you'll be coming.

Activity 2

Materials: none

Homework: Transfer Assignment 1 or 2, Materials Book, page 180 or 181, completed for an introduction

Directions: Follow the same procedure as in Activity 1, but role-play being the student's parent and have him introduce the people listed to the parent.

principal	teacher
coach	friend
music teacher	dance teacher
friend's parent	school nurse
school secretary	P.E. teacher

Activity 3

Materials: none

Homework: Transfer Assignment 1 or 2, Materials Book, page 180 or 181, completed for an introduction

Directions: Tell the student, "Sometimes you have to introduce yourself. Let's pretend we don't know each other. I want you to use your target behaviors and say, 'Excuse me,' or 'Hi! I'm ____. What's your name?'"

Tell the student that you'll pretend to be many different people and he can introduce himself to all of them.

Activity 4

Materials: play phones, Teletrainer® unit (Bell Telephone), inter-office extensions, or real phones

Homework: Transfer Assignment 1 or 2, Materials Book, page 180 or 181, completed for phone calls

Directions: Tell the student, "Sometimes phone calls are hard because we feel pressured to go fast. Also, there are no visual cues (gestures or facial expressions to help the listener), so all of our message comes from speech. We're going to practice using easy speech as we make phone calls. We'll begin by using pretend phones. Then, I'll get on the office extension and you can practice calling me. I'll show you how. I'll use (target behavior) when I talk on the phone. I'll say, 'Hi. This is Mrs. Corn. Is (student's name) there?' What target behaviors will you practice?" For students using word-initiation techniques, you might want to select a question to ask and decide on the technique(s) to use.

After you've practiced calling each other, have the student help you make a list of other people you could pretend to call. Have the student create a hierarchy for the order of practice. Then, pretend to be the other people and have the student call and ask for information, invite you to a party, give you a message, ask you for permission to do something, ask you to do him a favor, or place an order. Encourage the student to begin all calls by identifying himself by name as this gives additional practice in introductions.

Early in role-playing, be a good listener. Later, tell the student that you'll sometimes be a difficult listener. Tell the student you'll ask questions, misunderstand so he has to repeat, say you can't hear so he has to talk louder, say you have the wrong number, etc. Tell the student not to let you upset him or make him forget to use easy speech.

Familiar People and Topics

- parents: ask to bring your field trip permission
- coach: ask when and where practice is
- dance teacher: cancel lesson
- grandmother: ask to spend the night
- friend: ask for homework assignment
- neighbor: ask to buy candy for band
- grandpa: ask to supper
- aunt: give message from your mom
- teacher: invite to dance recital
- cousin: ask permission to borrow tent for weekend

Unfamiliar People and Topics

- phone operator: ask for information
- restaurant: ask hours and prices
- pharmacy: ask for medicines, baseball cards, glue, poster board, folders, crayons
- donut shop: ask for hours and prices
- ice cream shop: ask for hours and prices and flavor of the week
- bowling alley: ask for hours, prices, if lanes are open
- skating rink: ask for hours, prices, rentals
- library: ask for a book or video
- pizza parlor: order a pizza

Activity 5

Materials: real phones

Homework: Transfer Assignment 1 or 2, Materials Book, page 180 or 181, completed for a phone call

Directions: Tell the student, "Now, it's time to practice real calls. I'll go first. I'll use (target behavior). Listen. I'll practice what I want to say first. Then, I'll make the call."

Make the call. Then, say, "Now, it's your turn. Decide what you want to say and how. Now, practice it with me." Wait. "Now, let's do the real call." When beginning real calls, have the student ask simple questions such as:

- How late are you open?
- When do you open?
- When do you close?
- Are you open on Saturday?

Be sure to remind the student to say "Hello. My name is ____. (How late are you open?) Thank you." Select places where people are likely to be polite and patient, like a bank. Work up to harder places like a fast-food restaurant at a busy time.

Activity 6

Materials: real phones

Homework: none

Directions: Tell the student, "Sometimes you need to answer the phone, too. We'll role-play you getting a phone call. We'll both practice our target behaviors. First, I'll be me. Later, I'll pretend to be other people."

After the student has achieved success role-playing, try inter-office calls and have the student answer when you call him. Finally, if it's agreeable to the family, arrange a time for you to call the student several times at home so he gets practice answering calls in the home situation.

Activity 7

Materials: Fast-food Menu or Family Dining Menu, Materials Book, page 206 or 207 (or real menus from area restaurants)

Homework: Transfer Assignment 1 or 2, completed for role-playing ordering in a restaurant, and Fast-food Menu or Family Dining Menu, Materials Book, pages 180 or 181 and 206 or 207

Directions: Tell the student that you need to practice using easy speech to order in a restaurant. Have the student make a list of his favorite places to eat and arrange them in a practice hierarchy. Be sure to include a variety of places (e.g., fast-food, donut shop, cafeteria, family restaurant, school chili supper, ice cream store, pizza parlor, drive-up window, quick-stop shop, snack bar at ball park, sports food vendor, fancy restaurant).

Role-play being the food server and have the student role-play a restaurant ordering situation. Initially, be a good listener, but after the student has achieved success, add disrupters to the role-playing (e.g., ask the student to repeat, misunderstand what he says, ask to speak louder, interrupt with a question, bring the wrong items, etc.). Then, invite other people to join the session and role-play restaurant situations with them.

Activity 8

Materials: Permission Slip, Materials Book, page 155

Homework: Transfer Assignment 1, Materials Book, page 180, completed for a restaurant ordering task

Directions: Tell the student, "Now, we're going to go on a field trip to a restaurant so you can practice your easy speech there. We'll role-play what we'll say on the way. When we get there, would you like me to go first so you can hear me use easy speech or do you want to go first? I'll use (target behavior) on my turn." Go to various eating places and order food or drinks.

Activity 9

Materials: none

Homework: none

Directions: Tell the student, "Sometimes we have to get someone's attention. Sometimes that means raising our voices. Sometimes it means interrupting someone. Sometimes we have to speak quickly, too. It can be hard to remember easy speech at those times so we need to practice. Let's pretend you need to get someone's attention. Remember to use easy speech. What will you concentrate on doing?"

Role-playing Situations

Home

- calling to a parent when you get home
- calling to a parent to tell there's a phone call
- calling to your dad to come to dinner
- calling to your mom to say washer is overflowing

School

- getting a teacher's attention to tell that a bee is in the room
- calling to a friend to wait for you after school
- yelling a message to a friend across the playground
- calling to the bus driver to wait for you

Community

- getting a clerk's attention to ask for an item
- getting a stranger's attention to ask for directions
- yelling to a vendor that you want a drink at a ball park
- getting the librarian's attention to ask where the pay phone is

Invite other people to join the session and role-play some of these situations.

Activity 10

Materials: Jokes 1 or 2, Materials Book, page 208 or 209

Homework: Jokes 1 or 2, Materials Book, page 208 or 209

Directions: Tell the student, "Sometimes it's hard to remember easy speech when telling jokes so let's practice our target behaviors. I'll use (target behavior) on my turn. What will you use?"

Later, invite other people into the session or go around the building and tell the jokes to other people. Since both you and the student will be participating in the jokes, the student will have your model to help remind him of the target behaviors.

You might also consider videotaping a "program" in which you and the student tell the jokes (e.g., a comedy team) which you then could play for others. Or, you could present a comedy routine together for invited guests. You could also incorporate riddles from the Materials Book, pages 107 - 109, into this activity.

Activity 11

Materials: none

Homework: Transfer Assignment 1 or 2, Materials Book, page 180 or 181, completed for a greeting or departing practice

Directions: Tell the student, "It's important to practice easy speech all the time. We can practice as we greet or leave people. Let's pretend you just came into the room. We'll use our target behaviors as we greet each other." Wait. "Now, let's pretend it's time to go. What target behaviors can we practice as we say, 'Good-bye. See you tomorrow.'?" Practice the departing phrases.

"Let's make a list of other people you greet and leave. Then, we can role-play using easy speech with each other." Include some variations such as walking down the hall and greeting someone in passing, yelling a greeting or farewell across the playground, or meeting someone at the mall.

After the student has been successful in role-playing with you, invite others to the session to role-play. Then, go around the building and greet other people. To make this realistic, combine with other objectives such as taking a poll.

Activity 12

Materials: a pad or paper and pencil

Homework: Transfer Assignment 1, Materials Book, page 180, filled out with message for student to give home support person

Directions: Tell the student, "We can practice easy speech while taking and giving messages. If someone gives you a message, you should repeat the message to make sure it's right. That's a good time to practice your target behaviors. Then, when you give the message to someone, you can practice your target behaviors again.

"Let's pretend I have a message for your mother. After I give it to you, repeat it to me. 'Tell your mother that the open house is tomorrow at six o'clock.' What was the message?" Wait. "Now, I'll pretend I'm your mother. Give me the message." If the student is old enough, have him write the message down.

Have the student help you make a list of people who might give him a message for someone else. Use the list to set up role-playing situations like the following:

- from you to the school secretary
- from a friend to the friend's mother
- from the doctor to the student's parent
- from the dentist's receptionist to the student's parent
- from the student's grandfather to his father
- from the student's sister or brother to his parents
- from a neighbor to the student's parent
- from the mail carrier to the student's parent
- from an uncle to a cousin

Note: These types of situations may also be practiced using the phone.

After the student has practiced, give incomplete messages and have the student ask questions to clarify. For example, tell the event, but not the time or place. Remind the student to use easy speech when asking for the needed information.

Activity 13

Materials: notepad and pencil

Homework: Transfer Assignment 1 or 2, Materials Book, page 180 or 181, completed to role-play taking orders

Directions: Tell the student, "Sometimes we need to sell things or ask for donations to help raise money. We can practice easy speech while we do that. Let's pretend you're selling pizzas for your school. Pretend to knock on my door and then, ask me to buy some pizzas. Begin by telling me your name, what you're selling, and why. Then, ask me if I want to order some pizzas. I might ask some questions. If I decide to order, be sure to get my name, phone number, and address. Remember to use your target behaviors."

For a student who is using word-initiation modifications, you might think ahead and pick certain words on which to use specific techniques. For example, the student might plan ahead to use bouncing on "pizza" and sliding on all the "wh-" words.

After the student achieves success, invite others to join the session and role-play with them. You could also pretend to take orders over the phone.

Activity 14

Materials: can or container for collecting money

Homework: none

Directions: Tell the student, "Sometimes we have to collect money for charities. This can be hard because we have to start conversations with people we don't know. We can do it, though, if we remember to use easy speech. Let's pretend so you can get practice in using easy speech. Let's pretend I'm going into a store. Ask me if I want to donate money to (name a charity). Be sure to thank me even if I am unable to make a contribution. Remember to use your target behaviors."

After the student achieves success, invite others to join the session so you can role-play with them. To make the situation harder, ask the student to repeat or ask questions about what the money will be used for.

Activity 15

Materials: Invitations, Materials Book, page 210

Homework: Invitations, Materials Book, page 210

Directions: Cut the invitations apart. Tell the student, "Today we're going to practice easy speech while we pretend to invite each other to different events." Place the invitation cards on the table. Take turns picking a card and inviting each other. Tell the student, "Be sure to use your target behaviors as you give the information or tell me why you can or can't come. I may ask questions so be ready." Also, tell the student that you may not give enough information on your turn so he should be ready to ask you questions about time, place, what to wear, what to bring, etc.

After the student achieves success, invite others to join the session and role-play with them. You could also practice giving invitations over the phone. For real-life practice, invite people in the building to attend a session. You could also invite family members to attend a session.

> **Objective 3:** The student will use easy speech while expressing feelings.

Procedure

In this objective, the student will practice easy speech in activities which focus on the pragmatic function of expressing feelings. The student will role-play expressing feelings with you and then you'll invite others to join the session so the student can practice more realistic situations. Continue to assign home practice. Have the student help select activities and plan outside practice activities. Review the home and school information lists (Use lists from *The Fluency Companion* or create your own.) for ideas to make the transfer process fit the needs of each particular student. The information will help determine the kinds of activities in which your student participates that you can then emphasize in role-playing.

Model the tasks using the target behaviors as appropriate for the student (e.g., forward flowing speech, word-initiation techniques, or both) and then encourage the student to participate in the activities and use the target behaviors, too. For the student who has followed Path 1, encourage forward flowing speech. For students in Path 2 or 3, use word-initiation techniques or both word-initiation techniques and forward flowing speech as preparatory sets. If the latter students have difficulty, encourage them to use cancellations and pull-outs.

Activities in this objective target the pragmatic function of expressing feelings associated with:

- stating preferences
- talking about emotional topics
- congratulating
- giving and responding to compliments
- expressing thanks
- apologizing
- discussing stuttering
- responding to teasing

Activity 1

Materials: Preference Pictures 1 or 2, Materials Book, page 211 or 212

Homework: Preference Pictures 1 or 2, Materials Book, page 211 or 212

Directions: Cut the pictures apart. Place the pictures in a pile facedown. Tell the student, "Sometimes we have to tell people what we like and dislike. Let's practice easy speech while we take turns doing that. I'll show you first. I pick this card. I'll use (target behavior) while I tell you which one I like better. Then, it will be your turn."

After the student is successful at stating preferences, make it harder by telling the student that you'll disagree and he'll need to give more reasons for his preference. Let the student know that you're just pretending to disagree to give him more practice talking in easy speech.

Activity 2

Materials: none

Homework: Transfer Assignment 1 or 2, Materials Book, page 180 or 181, completed to role-play stating a preference

Directions: Tell the student, "Today, we're going to role-play some situations in which you have to state a preference. Remember to use easy speech." After the student is successful, invite others to join the session and role-play some of the situations.

Role-playing Situations

School
- The student tells the librarian which book he prefers.
- The student tells his coach which bat he prefers.
- The student tells his music teacher which song he prefers to play.
- The student tells a friend which game he prefers.
- The student tells the band director which instrument he prefers to play.
- The student tells his gym teacher which game he prefers to play at recess.
- The student tells his teacher which place he prefers to visit on a field trip.

Home
- The student tells a parent which shoes he prefers.
- The student tells a grandparent which dessert he prefers.
- The student tells a parent which bike he prefers.
- The student tells a sibling which TV show he prefers to watch.
- The student tells a cousin which movie he prefers to see.
- The student tells a grandparent which toy he prefers for a present.

Community
- The student tells the librarian which bookmark he prefers.
- The student tells the speech-language pathologist which reinforcement (e.g., sticker) he prefers.
- The student tells the food server which pizza he prefers.
- The student tells the food server which dessert he prefers.
- The student tells the fast-food clerk which drink he prefers.

After the student succeeds using easy speech in stating a simple preference, expand the role-playing by asking "why" and engaging in a conversation on the topic.

Activity 3

Materials: none

Homework: none

Directions: Tell the student, "Today we're going to practice easy speech while talking about our preferences." Have the student express his likes and dislikes as well as the reasons for them. Present a model by discussing your preferences, too. Have the student verbalize why you're having these discussions (e.g., to practice easy speech) as well as the target behaviors you'll be using.

Topics

- kinds of restaurants (fast-food, Mexican, Italian, Chinese)
- kinds of movies (science fiction, mystery, space, comedy)
- kinds of books (mystery, biography, animal)
- kinds of games (computer, board, card)
- kinds of television shows (comedy, game, talk, movies)
- kinds of sports (individual or team)

Activity 4

Materials: Emotional Pictures, Materials Book, page 213

Homework: Emotional Pictures, Materials Book, page 213

Directions: Cut the pictures apart. Place the cards in a pile on the table. Tell the student, "Sometimes it's hard to remember easy speech when you're talking about emotional topics. Let's see if you can remember to use your target behaviors while telling how you think the people on these cards feel. We can take turns. I'll use the target behaviors, too. First, I'll describe the picture and then I'll tell how I think the person feels."

Engage the student in conversation about the topic on the card. Ask if the student has ever had the same or a similar experience. Model the expression of your own feelings and experiences, too.

123

At this time it's likely the student may express some feelings about stuttering if he did not do so earlier. Discuss the feelings openly and consider options for dealing with the feelings. Some ideas are presented in the Branching Activity on page 128.

Activity 5

Materials: any Emotional Situation, Sequence, or Rebus Story, Materials Book, pages 157 - 172

Homework: none

Directions: Show the student the story. Say, "Remember this story? Has anything like this ever happened to you?" Remind the student to use easy speech. Model some of your own feelings and experiences, too.

Activity 6

Materials: none

Homework: none

Directions: Take turns talking about how you'd feel in the situations listed below. Say, "I want you to practice easy speech while you tell me how you would feel if these things happened to you."

Situations

- You broke your mother's favorite vase.
- You forgot your homework.
- You lost your lunch money.
- You missed your music lesson.
- Your friend has a new friend.
- Your father is sick.
- Your teacher accused you of throwing paper when you didn't.
- You have to stay after school for talking.
- Your stepmom had a new baby.
- Your mother won't buy you the outfit you want.
- You spilled spaghetti all over yourself at lunch.
- You tore the back of your pants.
- You tripped over someone's book bag and everyone laughed.
- You forgot to brush your hair.

- You tore your math book.
- Your grandfather had to go to the hospital.
- You got a bike for your birthday.
- Your friend got hurt.
- Your pet got lost or was killed.
- You wore two different socks to school.
- You forgot your umbrella on a rainy day.
- Your aunt gave you a new puppy.
- Your backpack is stolen.
- Your bike has a flat tire.
- Your coach made you run extra laps.
- You won a trophy.
- You lost a contest.
- You found five dollars.
- You got an A on a test.
- You were the last one picked to play ball.
- Your teacher picked you to take a message to the office.

After the student succeeds in using easy speech while discussing the above situations, try role-playing the situations. Invite others to join the session and role-play the situations with them, too.

Activity 7

Materials: none

Homework: none

Directions: Tell the student, "Sometimes we want to congratulate people. We can use easy speech when we say congratulations. Let's pretend I'm your coach and I just won the Coach of the Year Award. Use your target behaviors as you pretend to congratulate me." If the student only uses one word, model a longer response. "Hi, Coach. I just heard you won the Coach of the Year Award. That's great! Congratulations. Did you get a trophy?"

Role-play the situations below with the student congratulating the person listed. After the student is successful, invite others to join the session and role-play the situations with them.

Role-playing Situations

- a teacher being on TV
- a relative getting engaged
- a sibling graduating
- a sibling passing a driver's test
- a classmate winning a spelling bee
- a friend winning a race
- a teammate getting a hit
- father finishing a project
- mother getting a new job
- baby-sitter winning a vacation trip
- someone catching a big fish
- a friend winning an election

Activity 8

Materials: none

Homework: Transfer Assignment 1, Materials Book, page 180, completed for the student to compliment someone

Directions: Tell the student, "Let's practice easy speech while we pretend to give and receive compliments. Let's pretend I'm your grandma. Tell me you like my new hairstyle. Use your target behaviors. I'll use them, too, when I respond."

Have the student help you think of other people he could compliment and then role-play those situations. Also, tell the student you'll pretend to be other people and compliment him, so the student can practice easy speech in responding to compliments.

Role-playing Situations

Student compliments others

> your mom's new dress
>
> a friend's backpack
>
> your dad's new shirt
>
> the teacher's new hairstyle
>
> a friend's new toy
>
> your sister's new shoes
>
> your brother's drawing
>
> your aunt's dinner
>
> your grandpa's tie
>
> your coach's new cap

People compliment student

> Your stepmom says you look nice.
>
> Your dad says you did well in school.
>
> The teacher says you were a big help after school.
>
> The principal says you were polite on the field trip.
>
> Your coach says you got a good hit.
>
> Your music teacher says you played the song perfectly.
>
> A friend says your new shirt is cool.
>
> The secretary says you always have a happy smile.

After the student is successful, invite others to join the session and role-play the situations with them.

Activity 9

Materials: none

Homework: Transfer Assignment 1, Materials Book, page 180, completed for expressing thanks

Directions: Role-play thanking people. Have the student practice easy speech Say, "Let's pretend someone helps you do something. Use your easy speech as you tell them thanks. What would you say if I gave you a sticker?"

If the student only responds with one word, encourage the student to say what he's thankful for so he can get more practice using easy speech. Use the following suggestions for practice situations or have the student think of other times he might want to thank someone.

Role-playing Situations

Thank someone for:

- giving you a present
- giving you a compliment
- making you a snack
- giving you some money
- helping you make your bed
- inviting you to a party
- inviting you to join a club
- sharing lunch

- returning your lost pet
- giving you a message
- helping you wash your dog
- helping you change the litter box
- helping you open the window
- helping you take out the garbage
- helping you practice your spelling words
- helping you wrap a present

Activity 10

Materials: none

Homework: none

Directions: Tell the student, "We all have to apologize sometimes. Usually when we do, we're upset because we did something wrong. It's a time when we should use our easy speech. Let's role-play apologizing. Let's pretend you spilled milk on the rug. What will you say?" Use the suggested situations or have the student help you think of other situations to practice.

Role-playing Situations

- You lost your friend's book.
- You broke your dad's tape measure.
- You spilled juice on your mother's grocery list.
- You forgot to clean the chalkboard.
- You forgot to feed your dog.
- You stepped on the coach's foot.
- You bumped into someone in the mall.
- You forgot to call your grandma.

After the student is successful with you, invite others to join the session and role-play making apologies with them.

Activity 11

Materials: none

Homework: none

Directions: Tell the student, "Sometimes it's hard to remember to use easy speech when talking about stuttering. It's good to tell people about stuttering, so let's practice easy speech while we talk about

127

stuttering. Let's pretend you have to give a speech about yourself and your stuttering. Here's what you might say:

> (Model the target behaviors as you give a sample speech.) 'My name is ____. Sometimes I stutter, but I'm learning easy speech in speech class. Stuttering is when you hold out a sound or word like this (demonstrate a prolongation) or repeat a sound or word in a hard way like this (demonstrate a repetition) or get stuck on a word like this (demonstrate a silent block). I'm learning to easy talk by using (state/demonstrate the target behaviors being used). Stuttering isn't bad. It's just a different way of talking. I hope this helps you understand stuttering.'

"Now, you give a little speech like that. Remember to use easy speech."

After the student experiences success, invite others to the session and have the student give a speech about stuttering to them. Some students may want to include other information or to discuss teasing. To help guide the student in ways to express himself, follow the directions for the following activity.

Activity 12

Materials: none

Homework: none

Discussion: Tell the student that sometimes it's hard to use easy speech when responding to teasing. Discuss ways to respond to any kind of teasing. For example, ignore it, comment on it (e.g., "You're right. That was a silly thing to do."), laugh about it (e.g., "I sure felt silly when I spilled the pop all over me."), ask the teaser why she said what she said, or ask the person to stop (e.g., "I don't like it when you say things like that. I want you to stop."). Create some situations in which people tease each other and practice responding in different ways.

If the student seems to need to discuss teasing related to stuttering, do so and apply the above responses to different situations related to stuttering experiences. Role-play situations in which the different responses may or may not be appropriate.

Branching Activity

Materials: Feelings Analysis, Materials Book, page 214

Homework: none

Directions: Tell the student, "Sometimes it's a good idea to talk about how we feel about things." Then, use the Feelings Analysis activity sheet to model how you could analyze your feelings. Be sure to model easy speech as you talk. Encourage the student to do so, too.

Note: The student may become more disfluent as she discusses these topics. Since it's important to bring feelings out into the open, let the student talk even if she is disfluent, but keep modeling easy speech. Return to an easier task when the discussion ends to help the student regain control.

This activity can progress in many ways. Basically, you want to discuss *how* you feel, *when* you feel that way, *why* you feel that way, and *what* you can do. Often it will be necessary to discuss how realistic your feelings are. Sometimes it's helpful to talk about times when you feel the opposite (e.g. afraid/not afraid, like to talk/prefer not to talk, don't mind being teased/feel bad when teased). Two examples follow. You and your student can create your own, too. While discussing the topic, fill in the Feelings Analysis sheet, Materials Book, page 214.

When I was young, I was afraid of dogs. My mom asked me when I was afraid and I said, "when I'm alone on my way to school or at the park." She asked why I was afraid and I said, "because they bark and it hurts my ears." She said, "Is that all?" I said, "No. I'm afraid they'll bite me, and I'm afraid if they're big they'll knock me down." My mom said, "You aren't afraid of Grandma's dog, are you?" I said, "No." My mom said, "Well, you do need to be careful of strange dogs, but you don't want to be afraid. Let's think of how we can help you. First, you need to know what to do around dogs. Let's read about that. Then, you need to get used to dogs. Let's go to the pet shop and see some dogs, big and little ones. Maybe we can even get a dog of our own."

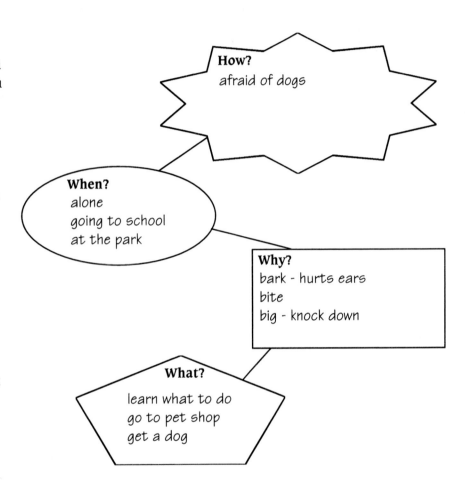

To do the opposite, you could fill out a chart of when you aren't afraid of dogs. In this instance, the "what" becomes "What makes me not afraid?"

A speech example follows. In this instance, you might discuss the concept of disclosure (e.g., people probably already know you stutter so there's not any need to hide it) and teasing. (Ways to discuss teasing are shared in Step 5, Activity 12, page 128.)

"You said you were afraid to give a speech. When are you afraid?" Wait. "At school, at church, and at scouts." Complete the chart. "Why?" Wait. "You're afraid because you might forget or because you might stutter. Why?" Wait. "Because everyone will laugh or tease you. Because they'll know you stutter."

Complete the chart. "Have you ever stuttered there (in class, at church, or scouts) before?" If yes, "Well then, they probably already know you stutter sometimes, don't they? Well, what can we do? Practice so you won't forget. Practice with easy talking."

Be specific regarding which target behaviors to use. "If people tease or laugh, have a plan for reacting such as ignoring them."

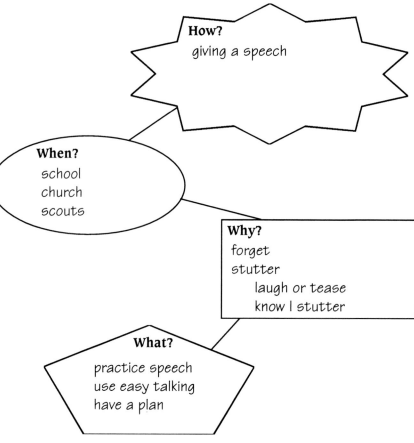

Modify this activity and the Feelings Analysis activity sheet to discuss many feelings including times when the student feels embarrassed, angry, or bothered by something. It can be especially useful in helping students work out how to deal with speech fears or concerns related to introductions, talking on the phone, ordering in a restaurant, reading out loud, or asking questions in class. Remember that completing the Feelings Analysis activity sheet for times when they aren't afraid or concerned as well as for those times when they are afraid or concerned can be helpful in addressing the key components of the situation.

Objective 4: The student will use easy speech while controlling.

Procedure

In this objective, the student practices easy speech in activities which focus on the pragmatic function of controlling. Have the student role-play controlling with you and then invite others to join the session so the student can practice more realistic situations. Continue to assign home practice. Have the student help select activities and plan outside practice activities. Review the home and school information lists (Use the lists in *The Fluency Companion* or create your own.) for ideas to make the transfer process fit the needs of each particular student. The information will help determine the kinds of activities in which your student participates that you can then emphasize in role-playing.

Model the tasks using the target behaviors as appropriate for the student (e.g., forward flowing speech, word-initiation techniques, or both) and then encourage the student to participate in the activities and use the target behaviors, too. For the student who has followed Path 1, encourage forward flowing speech. For students in Path 2 or 3, use word-initiation techniques or both word-initiation techniques and forward flowing speech as preparatory sets. If the latter students have difficulty, encourage them to use cancellations and pull-outs.

Activities in this objective target the pragmatic function of controlling associated with:

- asking for, giving, or refusing permission
- giving directions
- giving warnings
- convincing
- negotiating
- making promises
- asking for assistance or favors

Activity 1

Materials: none

Homework: Transfer Assignment 1 or 2, Materials Book, page 180 or 181, completed for role-playing asking for permission

Directions: Tell the student, "Some people have a hard time remembering to use easy speech when they have to ask for permission to do something. Let's practice your target behavior(s) while you pretend to ask me for permission. Pretend you want permission to change your speech day from Tuesday to Wednesday. Be sure to tell me why you want the permission."

Tell the student, "Now, I'll pretend to be other people and we'll role-play other times you might have to ask for permission. First, though, tell me why we're pretending."

Role-playing Situations

School

- to call home
- to use the rest room
- to get a tissue
- to go to the library
- to sharpen a pencil
- to wash your hands
- to use the computer
- to feed the fish
- to clean the chalkboard

Home

- to skip dance practice
- to go skating
- to stay overnight at a friend's
- to buy a new toy
- to order a milk shake
- to go to summer camp
- to go to the mall
- to turn on the TV
- to stay up late
- to wear shorts to school

- to leave your boots at home
- to invite a friend to a movie
- to put stars on your bedroom ceiling
- to go to a party
- to camp out
- to bake cookies
- to make Kool-Aid®
- to paint your desk
- to have a piece of cake

After the student experiences success with you, invite others to join a session and role-play these situations with them.

Activity 2

Materials: Giving Direction Pictures, Materials Book, page 215

Homework: Giving Direction Pictures, Materials Book, page 215

Directions: Cut the pictures apart. Place the pictures on the table. Tell the student, "Today, we're going to practice easy speech while we pretend to give other people directions. Pick a picture. Pretend you're one of the students and I'm the other one. Tell me what to do. First, tell me which target behavior you'll practice while you tell me." If this is too hard, model how to give directions for the student first and then let the student try the next situation.

Activity 3

Materials: appropriate materials for giving directions for a project (e.g., building a shadow box, carving a pumpkin, or making an ice cream float)

Homework: none

Directions: After the student has been successful role-playing giving directions to you in Activity 2, provide materials for one of the projects and have the student tell you how to actually complete the project. Remind the student to practice easy speech.

Tell the student, "You've done a great job of giving me directions using easy speech. Now, I want you to practice with other people. The next time you come, I'll have some other people here and you can give them directions." Invite one or two other people (children or adults) to attend a session.

Giving Warnings

Activity 4

Materials: Warning Pictures, Materials Book, page 216

Homework: Warning Pictures, Materials Book, page 216

Directions: Cut the pictures apart. Place the pictures facedown on the table. Tell the student, "Sometimes it's hard to remember to use easy speech when giving a warning. Often, we have to say things quickly or loudly to get the other person's attention. We can still speak easily and use our target behavior(s). Let's practice. I'll go first. I'll use (target behavior) while I warn you not to run with a pencil." After you finish, tell the student to pick the next card and warn you.

Convincing

Activity 5

Materials: Preference Pictures 1 or 2, Materials Book, page 211 or 212

Homework: Preference Pictures 1 or 2, Materials Book, page 211 or 212

Directions: Place the preference pictures on the table. Tell the student that you want him to practice easy speech while trying to convince you about something. Explain that you may disagree or argue (even when you really agree) just so he can get more practice in using easy speech. Ask the student to select a preference picture and then convince you why one of the items is better than the other.

Negotiating

Activity 6

Materials: none

Homework: none

Directions: Tell the student, "Sometimes when we want to persuade someone, we have to negotiate, to offer to trade something, or promise to do something in return. Sometimes it's hard to remember easy speech when you're negotiating because you might be excited or in a hurry. Today, I want you to practice easy speech while you pretend to negotiate with me. First, I'll be me. Try to persuade me not to give you any homework tonight. You could negotiate by promising to do twice as much next time."

After the student has experienced success with you, pretend to be other people. Also, invite other people to join the session and role-play the situations with them.

Role-playing Situations

Home with parent
- If I can go to a movie, I'll . . .
- If I can stay up late, I'll . . .
- If I can sleep over at a friend's house, I'll . . .
- If I can go sledding, I'll . . .
- If I can go to summer camp, I'll . . .
- If you lend me money, I'll . . .
- If you increase my allowance, I'll . . .
- If I can get a job, I'll . . .
- If I can go to a rock concert, I'll . . .

Home with sibling
- If I can borrow your _____, I'll . . .
- If you lend me your _____, I'll . . .
- If you do my chores, I'll . . .

Friend
- If you lend me your _____, I'll . . .
- If you give me your dessert, I'll . . .
- If you let me go first, I'll . . .
- If you help me with my homework, I'll . . .

Activity 7

Materials: none

Homework: none

Directions: Tell the student, "Sometimes we have to make promises to people. Let's role-play making promises so we can practice easy speech. Pretend you want to play Go Fish®. Promise me you'll use easy speech if I let you play Go Fish®." Tell the student that you'll pretend to be other people so he can practice easy speech with others. Have the student help you think of role-playing ideas or use the ones listed below.

Role-playing Situations

Home promises

clean your room	turn down the radio
watch the baby	stop slamming the door
wash the dishes	pick up your clothes
do the laundry	put away the toys
weed the flowers	clean the pet cage

School promises

> bring back the library books
>
> return a permission slip
>
> feed the gerbil
>
> water the plants
>
> collect the lunch money
>
> meet a friend after school
>
> erase the chalkboard

Community promises

> clean litter from the bike path
>
> rake a neighbor's yard
>
> shovel a neighbor's walk
>
> feed a friend's pet
>
> collect cans of food for the food pantry

After the student has experienced success with you, invite other people to join the session and role-play with them.

Activity 8

Materials: Assistance Pictures, Materials Book, page 217

Homework: Assistance Pictures, Materials Book, page 217

Directions: Cut the pictures apart. Tell the student, "Today, we'll practice easy speech while we pretend to ask for assistance. I'll show you. I'll pick the first card. I need help so I'll use (target behavior) to ask you to help me. Then, you can pick the next card and ask me for help. What will you remember to practice on your turn?"

After the student has experienced success with you, invite others to join the session and role-play the situations with them.

Activity 9

Materials: Direction Pictures 1 or 2, Materials Book, page 120 or 121

Homework: Direction Pictures 1 or 2, Materials Book, page 120 or 121

Directions: Place the direction pictures on the table. Tell the student, "I'll pick a place. It's a drugstore. Now use easy speech and say, 'Ms. Allen, if you're going to the drugstore, would you do me a favor? I need some toothpaste. Could you get me some?'" Take turns picking places and asking favors.

After the student is successful, expand the interactions with some conversation.

Activity 10

Materials: Direction Pictures 1 or 2, Materials Book, page 120 or 121

Homework: Direction Pictures 1 or 2, Materials Book, page 120 or 121

Directions: Place the direction pictures on the table. Tell the student, "Today we'll offer a favor as we complete this task. Remember to use easy speech. Pick a place. Say, 'I'm going to the ____. Would you like me to get anything for you?' I'll answer. Sometimes I'll add some questions or make comments. Be ready to use your easy speech as we talk."

Also, spend some time just discussing when the student might ask for or offer assistance/favors. You could make a list of the times and role-play the situations.

> **Objective 5:** The student will use easy speech while imagining.

Procedure

In this objective, the student practices easy speech in activities which focus on the pragmatic function of imagining. In the preceding objectives, the student always played himself. Now, repeat any of the role-playing situations and have the student take on someone else's role. Also, you'll introduce some new activities designed just to elicit practice in imagining other characters' roles. You'll have the student role-play the imagining activities with you and then you'll invite others to join the session so the student can practice more realistic situations. Encourage the student to vary speech by using different pitches, loudness patterns, qualities, and rates. In this way, the student will gain confidence in his ability to control speech.

Continue to assign home and, whenever possible, school practice and involve the student in selecting activities and planning outside practice activities. Review the home and school information lists (Use the lists from *The Fluency Companion* or create your own.) for ideas to make the transfer process fit the needs of each particular student. The information will help determine the kinds of activities in which your student participates that you can then emphasize in role-playing.

Model the tasks using the target behaviors as appropriate for the student (e.g., forward flowing speech, word-initiation techniques, or both) and then encourage the student to participate in the activities and use the target behaviors, too. For the student who has followed Path 1, encourage forward flowing speech. For students in Path 2 or 3, use word-initiation techniques or both word-initiation techniques and forward flowing speech as preparatory sets. If the latter students have difficulty, encourage them to use cancellations and pull-outs.

Activities in this objective target the pragmatic function of imagining associated with:

- taking on roles of family members
- taking on roles of community workers
- taking on roles of famous people
- taking on roles of fictional characters
- taking on roles of historical characters
- creating original stories and dialogues
- creating original monologues

Activity 1

Materials: any Family Puppets, Materials Book, pages 187 - 190 (optional)

Homework: any Family Puppets, Materials Book, pages 187 - 190

Directions: Role-play any situations from Step 5, Objectives 1-4, pages 102 - 136, that involve family members. Have the student take on the family member's role. Tell the student, "I want you to pretend to be your (mother) and I'll be you. Let's pretend I want permission to spend the night with your best friend. Use easy speech when you tell me I can or cannot spend the night." You can use puppets or simply role-play the situation. Include tasks involving making promises, negotiating, convincing, stating preferences, clarifying, apologizing, giving permission, warning, asking for assistance, congratulating, etc.

Activity 2

Materials: toy phones or office extensions

Homework: none

Directions: Tell the student, "I want you to pretend to be your (stepfather). I'll pretend to be you. I'll call and ask you to bring my baseball glove to the ball park. You use easy speech when you talk to me. Try to think what your (stepfather) would say." Role-play several phone calls with the student taking on a family member's role.

Activity 3

Materials: any Community Worker Puppets, Materials Book, pages 191 - 194 (optional)

Homework: any Community Worker Puppets, Materials Book, pages 191 - 194

Directions: Cut apart the puppets. Tell the student, "Today, I want you to pretend to be a community worker and tell me all about your job. I want you to use easy speech while you tell me." Simply name a community worker or show the student the puppet for a visual cue.

Activity 4

Materials: any Family and Community Worker Puppets, Materials Book, pages 187 - 194 (optional)

Homework: any Family and Community Worker Puppets, Materials Book, pages 187 - 194

Directions: Cut apart the puppets. Tell the student, "Today, we're going to practice easy speech while we pretend some situations. I want you to be the community worker. Sometimes I'll be you and sometimes I'll be someone else. I'll use (target behavior) on my turn. What will you practice on your turn?" Either role-play situations from the list or use the puppets and create a puppet play. You might also have the student help you think of other situations.

Role-playing Situations

- dentist/patient: exam
- eye doctor/patient: need for glasses
- fire fighter/student: getting a cat down from a tree
- receptionist/parent: making an appointment
- police officer/student: bike safety
- grocer/parent: location of cat food
- nurse/patient: identifying information
- crossing guard/student: asking where to pick up your uniform
- pilot/passenger: discussing emergency procedures
- ticket agent/student: asking about prices and locations of seats
- hair stylist/student: asking about haircut
- librarian/student: talking about where to get information on dinosaurs
- mail carrier/student: asking about an expected package
- camp counselor/camper: talking about cooking over campfire

Activity 5

Materials: none

Homework: none

Directions: Tell the student, "I want you to practice easy speech while pretending to be a famous person. I'll interview you. Who is your favorite movie star or sports figure? Pretend to be that person. Before we start, tell me why we're pretending like this."

Activity 6

Materials: none

Homework: none

Directions: Tell the student, "I want you to practice easy speech while you pretend to be some of your favorite story characters. Let's make a list of characters you could pretend to be. Then, I'll interview you and you pretend to answer just like your character. Remember to use easy speech." Use the list below to get started.

Story Characters

Superman	Uncle Sam
Batman	Davy Crockett
Mary Poppins	Hercules
The Little Mermaid	Cinderella
Ramona Quimby	Aladdin

Activity 7

Materials: any Story Puppets, Materials Book, pages 195 - 198, or any puppet (optional)

Homework: any Story Puppets, Materials Book, pages 195 - 198 (optional)

Directions: Tell the student, "Let's act out some familiar stories. We can be different characters. Let's pretend we're Beauty and the Beast talking to each other. Which one do you want to be? Remember to use easy speech on your turn." Have the student suggest characters he would like to be.

You could also use the story puppets to create a puppet play. You will each have to do more than one part. Once the student experiences success with you, invite others to come to the session and put on the puppet show for them. Consider presenting it for a class of younger children (maybe kindergarten). You could also make a video of the puppet play and show it to others.

Activity 8

Materials: none

Homework: none

Directions: Tell the student, "Today, I want you to pretend to be a famous person in history. I'll pretend to interview you and you answer just like that person would. Be sure to practice easy speech." Have the student think of a famous person or select one from the list below.

Historical Figures

Mary Bethune	Ghandi
Thomas Jefferson	Ponce de Leon
Rosa Parks	Leonardo da Vinci
John Kennedy	Martin Luther King, Jr.
Paul Revere	Amelia Earhart
Betsy Ross	Louisa May Alcott
Clara Barton	Pocahontas
Florence Nightingale	George Washington
Booker T. Washington	Abraham Lincoln
Marco Polo	Chief Black Hawk

Activity 9

Materials: none

Homework: none

Directions: Tell the student, "Today, I want you to pretend to be a famous person in history. I'll be another famous person. We'll have a conversation. Who would you like to be?" Wait. "I think I'll be Betsy Ross. Now, we can practice easy speech while we talk. I'll concentrate on (target behavior). What will you concentrate on?"

Activity 10

Materials: any Matching Pictures or Memory Cards, Materials Book, pages 31 - 42 or pages 43 - 46

Homework: any Matching Pictures or Memory Cards, Materials Book, pages 31 - 42 or pages 43 - 46

Directions: Place the pictures in a pile. Take turns selecting three pictures. Tell the student, "I want you to make up a story using these three pictures. Be sure to use your easy speech. I'll go first and make up a story with these three pictures. I will use (target behavior). Then, it will be your turn."

After the student experiences success with you, invite others to join the session and have the student create original stories using easy speech.

Activity 11

Materials: any puppets from the Materials Book, pages 187 - 198

Homework: any puppets from the Materials Book, pages 187 - 198

Directions: Tell the student, "Today, we're going to select puppets and create a dialogue with them. We can do or say whatever we want. We just have to use the time to practice what?"

If desired, write a puppet play and invite people to come to see it. You could present it for another class or videotape it and show it to others.

Activity 12

Materials: any Unemotional or Emotional Situation, Sequence, or Rebus Story, Materials Book, pages 56 - 69 or 157 - 172

Homework: none

Directions: Look at the stories and work together with the student to create dialogues for the characters. Use easy speech while creating the dialogues. Then, act out the stories as a play or puppet play. Practice easy speech during the presentation. Later, present the play for others you invite to the session. You could also present the play to a classroom of younger students or make a videotape and show it to others.

Activity 13

Materials: any familiar fairy tale or tall tale

Homework: none

Directions: Model easy speech while you and the student create a new story by changing characters, locations, etc. Remind the student to use easy speech on this project. When completed, tell the story or act out the story using easy speech. Present the story or play to others.

Activity 14

Materials: Products, Materials Book, page 218

Homework: Products, Materials Book, page 218

Directions: Cut the pictures apart. Place the product pictures in a pile. Tell the student to pick a card. Then, say, "I want you to pretend you're advertising or giving a commercial for the product on the card. Practice your easy speech while you talk."

After the student experiences success with you, invite others to join the session and have the student present the commercial for them. You could also videotape the commercial and play it for others.

Activity 15

Materials:: any Community Worker Puppets, Materials Book, pages 191 - 194 (optional)

Homework: any Community Worker Puppets, Materials Book, pages 191 - 194 (optional)

Directions: Name a community worker or show the student a puppet of a community worker. Say, "Today, we're going to practice easy talking while pretending to be community workers. We'll pretend we've come to the classroom and we're going to tell all about ourselves. I'll go first. I'll pretend to be a fire fighter. I'll practice easy speech while I tell you what I do. When I'm done, you can pick a community worker and practice easy speech while you tell me what that community worker does."

Step 6: Maintaining

> **Goal:** The student will maintain gains made while gradually reducing direct therapy contacts.

The goal of this step is to phase out therapy by gradually decreasing direct contact with the student. While a specific progression is presented, it's important to develop a program to meet each student's needs. Continue to review the components involved in use of easy speech.

If you think the student should become involved with the National Stuttering Project and have not yet given the family information about it, consider doing so at this time. Discuss this idea with the parents first; if they are in agreement, then discuss it with the student. If the student and parent(s) feel it would be in the best interests of the student to become involved, share the following information:

National Stuttering Project
5100 E. La Palma Ave., Suite 208
Anaheim Hills, CA 92807

Telephone: 714-693-7480, 1-800-364-1677
Fax: 714-693-7554
e-mail: NSPmail@aol.com

Suggestions for Support Providers

Home and School

Share Home Letter 6 and School Letter 6, pages 164 and 165. These letters include general information about the maintenance program. Maintain contact as suggested.

What if significant others (e.g., teachers, parents) expect total fluency? It's important to remind them that total fluency is not the goal; no one is totally fluent. Briefly describe the difference between easy disfluencies and stuttering disfluencies as noted in Step 1.

What if the student begins to stutter more as direct therapy contacts are decreased? Is it always necessary to begin therapy again? By talking to the student's parent and/or the outside support people/teacher, it's often possible to identify and eliminate outside factors affecting fluency. It's also possible that increasing home and school activities will lead to increased fluency. If stuttering continues, however, it's wise to resume direct therapy as soon as possible.

Attitudes/Advocacy

Continue to review the attitudes introduced previously.

Objective 1: The student will maintain easy speech as direct therapy contacts are reduced to once a week.

Procedure

Continue Step 5 therapy, but only once a week.

A typical session consists of a review of the components of easy speech, a Step 2 or 3 activity to establish fluency, and then several transfer activities.

If the student is disfluent, reschedule therapy to two or three times a week. Use only Step 2 or 3 activities until fluency is regained. Then, reintroduce Step 4 and Step 5 activities and re-establish fluency before reducing therapy contacts again. If stuttering does not begin, continue therapy once weekly for four to six weeks; then, reduce therapy to twice a month.

Objective 2: The student will maintain easy speech as direct therapy contacts are reduced to twice a month.

Procedure

Continue Step 5 therapy twice a month for one to two months. Encourage parents/significant others to phone in a progress report during the weeks the student is not attending therapy. Also, maintain contact with the student's teachers to determine how the student is talking at school.

A typical session consists of reviewing the behaviors involved in using easy speech, a Step 2 or 3 activity to establish fluency, and then several transfer activities.

If the student is disfluent, reschedule therapy to once a week. Use only Step 2 or 3 activities until fluency is regained. Then, reintroduce Step 4 and Step 5 activities and re-establish fluency before reducing therapy contacts again. If the student is fluent, continue therapy twice a month for two months; then, reduce therapy to once a month.

Objective 3: The student will maintain easy speech as direct therapy contacts are reduced to once a month.

Procedure

Continue Step 5 therapy once a month for two months. Continue to encourage parents/significant others to phone in a progress report at least every other week. Also, continue to maintain contact with the teachers.

143

A typical session consists of a review of the behaviors involved in using easy speech, a Step 2 or 3 activity to establish fluency, and then several transfer activities.

If the student is disfluent, reschedule therapy to once or twice a week. Use only Step 2 or 3 activities until fluency is regained. Then, reintroduce Step 4 and Step 5 activities and re-establish fluency before reducing therapy contacts again. If the student is fluent, continue therapy once a month for two months; then, reduce therapy to once every three months.

Objective 4: The student will maintain easy speech as direct therapy contacts are reduced to one session in three months.

Procedure

Conduct Step 5 therapy for one session in three months. Continue to encourage parents/significant others to phone in a progress report periodically. Also, continue to maintain contact with teachers.

A typical session consists of reviewing the behaviors present in the use of easy speech, a Step 2 or 3 activity to establish fluency, and then several transfer activities.

If the student begins to stutter, reevaluate the student. If necessary, reinstate regular therapy sessions; the frequency and nature of the therapy will be dependent on the severity of the stuttering. After fluency has been regained, reduce therapy contacts once again. If stuttering doesn't return during the three-month break from therapy, dismiss the student, but arrange for a six-month recheck.

Objective 5: The student will maintain easy speech as direct therapy contacts are reduced to a six-month recheck.

Procedure

Dismiss the student, but arrange for a six-month recheck. Encourage the family and others involved with the student to contact you if stuttering begins again.

Objective 6: The student will maintain easy speech as activities provided by support personnel are reduced to once or twice a week.

Procedure

Instruct those involved with the student's therapy to continue to model easy speech, but to reduce direct practice to once or twice a week. If fluency is maintained, tell them to gradually decrease the activities to once a month.

Objective 7: The student will maintain easy speech as activities provided by support personnel are reduced to an "as needed" basis.

Procedure

Instruct the student, parent, and outside support people to continue to use easy speech, but to discontinue direct home or school assignments. Remind the support people to resume practice as needed to relax the student or to reduce general tension, particularly around holidays, vacations, birthdays, or when the student is ill, excited, or upset.

Home Letter A

Dear Family,

As you know, I'll be testing your child to see if there's a need to begin therapy for stuttering. If there is, I'll be sharing a number of letters with you regarding my therapy approach. Like many other parents, you may be wondering how you can help. There are many possibilities. First, learn as much as you can about stuttering. I'll share a lot of information and will direct you to other sources, too.

Second, create an atmosphere at home which encourages fluency development.

- Speak a little slower when talking with your child and pause often so your child realizes that speech doesn't have to be rushed.
- Refrain from interrupting, especially when your child is stuttering.
- Don't offer advice such as, "Stop and think" or "Take a deep breath" or "Relax."
- Maintain eye contact with your child.
- Don't convey concern, alarm, or disapproval when your child gets stuck on a word. Wait patiently and concentrate on *what* your child is saying and not on *how* your child is speaking.

Third, don't be afraid to discuss stuttering with your child. Your child is old enough to talk openly with you. In fact, it may be a great relief to your child. Talk about how some days are harder than others. Talk about how some people are better at some things than at other things and that includes speech.

Fourth, don't make stuttering the focus of your lives. Focus on the things your child does really well and give your child a lot of opportunities to achieve praise and success in these activities.

Fifth, accept your child's stuttering, not in the sense of not being able to do anything about it, but in the sense that at this time, it's part of who your child is. If you aren't embarrassed about your child's stuttering, maybe your child won't be embarrassed either. When your child is having a really bad time, help ease the tension with a comment like, "Wow! That was a really tough word."

Sixth, talk openly about your child's speech with family, relatives, and friends. Be an advocate for your child. Share the information I'll be giving you with others. You might even consider securing and distributing brochures from agencies like the Stuttering Foundation of America, 1-800-992-9392 or the National Stuttering Project 1-800-364-1677 or becoming involved in a support group.

Finally, if therapy is needed, you can help by becoming actively involved. I'll ask you for information about your child so I can personalize your child's therapy. I'll invite you to attend some sessions so you can observe and participate in our work. I'll also provide home assignments so you and your child can work together. In addition, I'll ask your permission to coordinate our work with your child's classroom teacher. With a coordinated home and school program, your child should make excellent progress.

I hope you find these suggestions helpful. If you have any questions, feel free to contact me.

Sincerely,

_____
Speech-Language Pathologist

School Letter A

Dear _____,

I'll be testing _____ to see if therapy for stuttering is necessary. Since many teachers often have questions about how to treat a child who stutters in the classroom, here are some suggestions which have been helpful to others.

First, you can help by providing a good speech model. Speak a little slower and pause often to create a relaxed communication atmosphere. Pause before responding to your students' questions so they won't feel rushed to respond quickly, too.

Second, create a good speech environment. Don't let your students interrupt each other and be sure everyone gets a chance to talk. Listen attentively to what is said rather than how it is said. Follow the student's lead in conversation. Speech is more likely to be fluent when a student is talking about something of personal interest. Avoid asking too many questions as they put the student on the spot and increase tension.

Third, while you should treat _____ the same as the other children, there are some extra things you can do to help. Call on students in random order, as a set order increases the anxiety level for the child who stutters. Try to call on the student who stutters more on fluent days and less on difficult days. In fact, it's usually easier for a student who stutters to respond when s/he volunteers than when called upon unexpectedly. If oral presentations are required, we can work together to find a way of making them less threatening.

Fourth, don't be afraid to discuss speech, but do so privately (or if you would be more comfortable, when I'm also present). Don't be embarrassed by the stuttering. Wait patiently, maintain eye contact, and concentrate on the content. How you respond will set the tone for how your other students respond. Perhaps you can take time (or we could do this together) to talk to your class about how we're all different and that we all deserve to be treated with respect.

Finally, if we begin therapy, I'll need your input regarding classroom activities to practice in therapy to make our sessions meaningful and practical. I'll share information often and would appreciate your feedback. If possible, I would also like to have you attend some sessions.

I hope you find these suggestions helpful. If you have questions or suggestions, please talk with me. A coordinated school program is essential to success. I appreciate your interest and support.

Sincerely,

_____
Speech-Language Pathologist

Home Letter 1

Dear Family,

I'm going to be meeting with your child to give him/her more information about the speech therapy program for stuttering. If your child is interested, s/he'll be starting therapy with me soon. The purpose of this letter is to tell you about the program.

The program involves six steps. During Step 1, your child will decide whether to enroll in the program to learn to use easy speech. The terms *fluency* and *disfluency* will be defined. Your child will learn that the goal of developing easy speech doesn't involve achieving perfect fluency — no one has perfect fluency. It's hard or stuttering disfluencies that cause problems in speech.

Next, your child will do some unison activities to help him/her use easy speech. Your child will also understand the other steps involved with the therapy program:

Step 2 — telling the difference between typical speech and stuttering
Step 3 — producing easy speech
Step 4 — using easy speech in the presence of disrupters
Step 5 — using easy speech in real-life situations
Step 6 — maintaining use of easy speech with fewer therapy contacts.

When we talk about the steps, I'll give your child a handout describing them. Then, your child will decide whether s/he wants to make a commitment to the therapy process. At this point, your input will be important. The task of changing stuttering to use of easy speech is not easy. If your child decides to make the commitment, s/he will have to work hard and progress will be slow. It's important that family members and others close to your child be involved with therapy. If your child makes a commitment to therapy, we'd like you to participate and also to provide input.

I'm looking forward to your child's decision. If your child decides to enroll, I look forward to continued contact with you.

Sincerely,

_____
Speech-Language Pathologist

School Letter 1

Dear _____,

I'm going to be meeting with _____ to give him/her more information about the speech therapy program for stuttering. If the student is interested, s/he'll be starting therapy with me soon. The purpose of this letter is to tell you about the program.

The program involves six steps. During Step 1, the student will be asked to determine if s/he will make a commitment to learning to use easy speech. The terms *fluency* and *disfluency* will be defined. The student will learn that the goal of developing easy speech does not involve achieving perfect fluency — no one has perfect fluency. It's hard or stuttering disfluencies that cause problems in speech.

Next, the student will do some unison activities to help him/her use easy speech. The student will also understand the other steps involved with the therapy program:

Step 2 — distinguishing typical speech from stuttering
Step 3 — producing easy speech
Step 4 — using easy speech in the presence of disrupters
Step 5 — using easy speech in real-life situations
Step 6 — maintaining use of easy speech with fewer therapy contacts.

When we talk about the steps, the student will receive a handout describing the steps. Then, the student will decide whether s/he wants to make a commitment to the therapy process. At this point, your input will be important. The task of changing stuttering to use of easy speech is not easy. If the student decides to make the commitment, s/he will have to work hard and progress will be slow. It's important that family members as well as school personnel close to the student become involved with therapy. If the student makes a commitment to therapy, we'd like you to participate and also to provide input.

I'm looking forward to the student's decision. If s/he decides to enroll, I look forward to continued contact with you.

Sincerely,

_____
Speech-Language Pathologist

Home Letter 2

Dear Family,

Now that your child has made a commitment to therapy, I'd like to share important information about Step 2, Analyzing. During this step, we'll define and model both easy disfluencies and stuttering disfluencies.

All of us have easy disfluencies. Some examples of easy disfluencies are:

- Revisions — starting to talk, stopping, and then starting over again ("I walked — no I ran to the store.")
- Interjections — adding extra sounds or words while we're thinking ("I wanted some candy — um — to eat at the movie, but I — well — I didn't — you know — have any money.")
- Whole word repetitions of only one or two times ("I-I-I did know your name, but but I forgot it.")
- Phrase repetitions — repeating two or three words at a time ("And then, and then, and then she hit the ball really far!")
- Hesitations — short, relaxed pauses between words ("I told [pause] my teacher that I forgot [pause] my homework.")

When disfluencies are no longer easy, but are tense and hard, these are stuttering disfluencies or stuttering. Examples of stuttering disfluencies are:

- Multiple whole-word repetitions — saying a word over and over again often in a tense, irregular rhythm ("I-I-I-I-I-I don't want to.")
- Part-word repetitions — repeating part of a word, sound, or syllable over and over again ("I li-li-li-li-li-li-like it.")
- Prolongations — holding on to a sound for too long a time ("N——————-o, it's m————-ine.")
- Silent blocks — attempting to push speech out, but nothing comes out because there's a lot of tension ("I [silent block] can't find him.")

During this step, your child will study disfluencies in my speech, in her/his speech, and in the speech of other people. I hope that you'll be able to attend a session soon to observe our work. I'll be contacting you for the best time.

If you have any questions, please contact me. Meanwhile, I want you to know that I'm enjoying the time I'm spending with your child!

Sincerely,

_____
Speech-Language Pathologist

School Letter 2

Dear _____,

Now that _____ has made a commitment to therapy, I'd like to share important information about Step 2, Analyzing. During this step, both easy disfluencies and stuttering disfluencies will be defined and modeled.

All of us have easy disfluencies. Some examples of easy disfluencies are:

- Revisions — starting to talk, stopping, and then starting over again ("I walked — no I ran to the store.")
- Interjections — adding extra sounds or words while we're thinking ("I wanted some candy — um — to eat at the movie, but I — well — I didn't — you know — have any money.")
- Whole word repetitions of only one or two times ("I-I-I did know your name, but but I forgot it.")
- Phrase repetitions — repeating two or three words at a time ("And then, and then, and then she hit the ball really far!")
- Hesitations — short, relaxed pauses between words ("I told [pause] my teacher that I forgot [pause] my homework."

When disfluencies are no longer easy, but are tense and hard, these are stuttering disfluencies or simply stuttering. Examples of stuttering disfluencies are:

- Multiple whole-word repetitions — saying a word over and over again often in a tense, irregular rhythm ("I-I-I-I-I-I don't want to.")
- Part-word repetitions — repeating part of a word, a sound, or a syllable over and over again ("I li-li-li-li-li-like it.")
- Prolongations — holding on to a sound for too long a time ("N———————-o, it's m————-ine.")
- Silent blocks — attempting to push speech out, but nothing comes out because there's a lot of tension ("I [silent block] can't find him.")

During this step, the student will analyze disfluencies in my speech, in her/his speech, and in the speech of other people. I hope you'll be able to attend a session soon to observe our work. I'll be contacting you to arrange a good time.

If you have any questions, please contact me.

Sincerely,

_____
Speech-Language Pathologist

Home Letter 3.1A

Dear Family,

Your child continues to climb up the steps to easy speech. We're now ready to learn how to produce forward flowing speech. When producing forward flowing speech, we'll use a slower rate than we usually use and we'll run the words together.

I'll show your child how to produce forward flowing speech. We'll practice it in unison and then in imitation. Because this is a new way of talking for your child, we'll need to practice it a lot. We'll practice forward flowing speech in:

- stereotyped sentences: "I pick a card. I need it. Your turn."
- in carrier sentences: "I found a _____, I need a _____, I want a _____, This is a _____."
- questions and answers
- simple sentences we make up

To make the practice fun, we'll use many games and activities in which we can use these types of sentences.

We'll invite you to a session soon so we can demonstrate how to do forward flowing speech. That way you'll know what to expect when your child brings home practice materials. Your support and encouragement will help your child learn this new way of talking.

If you have any questions, please contact me. Your input is of great value to us.

Sincerely,

_____
Speech-Language Pathologist

School Letter 3.1A

Dear _____,

_____ continues to climb up the steps to easy speech. We're now ready to learn how to produce forward flowing speech. When producing forward flowing speech, we'll use a slower rate than we usually use and we'll run the words together.

I'll show your student how to produce forward flowing speech. We'll practice it in unison and then in imitation. Because this is a new way of talking, we'll need to practice it a lot. We'll practice forward flowing speech in:

- stereotyped sentences: "I pick a card, I need it, Your turn"
- carrier sentences: "I found a _____, I need a _____, I want a _____, This is a _____."
- questions and answers
- simple sentences we make up

To make the practice fun, we'll use many games and activities in which we can use these types of sentences.

We'll invite you to a session soon so we can demonstrate how to do forward flowing speech. We can also discuss ways you can give _____ practice with structured responses in your classroom activities. Your support and encouragement will be extremely helpful.

If you have any questions, please contact me. Your input is of great value to us.

Sincerely,

_____
Speech-Language Pathologist

Home Letter 3.1B

Dear Family,

As you know, your child has been learning forward flowing speech. Sometimes it's hard to learn forward flowing speech all at once. To help, we slow speech down and then gradually speed it back up. We do this by teaching what we call *prolonged speech*. This is what your child and I will be working on for the next few sessions.

We'll begin by learning super slow speech. This speech is so slow you can only say two or three words on a breath. In addition to talking slowly, we'll stress running the words together. I'll call this *dragged-out speech* or *stretched-out speech* to help your child understand. Your child will only use this speech with me. It's much too slow to be generally accepted. The purpose is to go very slowly at first to gain a sense of control.

Next, we'll practice medium slow speech. At this rate, you can say four to five words on a breath. Your child will use this speech, too, only in the speech room. We'll concentrate on rate control and running the words together in a forward flowing manner.

Then, we'll practice slightly slow speech (which is really the same as forward flowing speech). Once your child can produce this rate, we'll practice it in structured activities so that this type of speech becomes a new habit for speech production. Before moving into the activities, though, we'll spend a little time just switching from super slow to slightly slow rates to give your child an even greater sense of control over speech production.

Your child will bring home activity sheets describing this process and we'll invite you to attend a session to see how we practice. There won't be any home assignments until we begin practicing forward flowing speech.

If you have questions, please contact me. I'm grateful for your interest and support.

Sincerely,

_____
Speech-Language Pathologist

School Letter 3.1B

Dear _____,

As you know, _____ and I have been learning forward flowing speech. Sometimes it's hard to learn forward flowing speech all at once. To make it easier, we teach prolonged speech by slowing speech way down and then gradually speeding it back up. We'll be working on prolonged speech for the next few sessions.

First, we'll learn super slow speech. This speech is so slow a person can only say two to three words on a breath. In addition to talking slowly, we'll also run the words together for dragged out speech or stretched out speech. We'll use this speech just in the speech room because it's much too slow to be generally accepted. By speaking so slowly, we'll develop a sense of control and of moving forward in speech production.

Next, we'll practice medium slow speech. At this rate a person can say four to five words on a breath. This speech, too, will only be used in the speech room. We'll concentrate on rate control and running the words together in a forward flowing manner.

Then, we'll practice slightly slow speech (which is really the same as forward flowing speech). We'll resume our structured practice activities so that this type of speech becomes a firm new habit for speech production. Before moving into the activities, though, we'll spend a little time switching from super slow to slightly slow rates just to give _____ an even greater sense of control over speech production.

If you have questions, please contact me. I'm grateful for your interest and support.

Sincerely,

_____
Speech-Language Pathologist

Home Letter 3.2A

Dear Family,

I'm enjoying working with your child. The focus of our work is on learning to use easy speech. Sometimes getting a word started is hard so I'll be showing your child four ways to start a word in an easy, relaxed, forward flowing manner. Your child will bring home activity sheets describing the rules for each technique, and I'll invite you to join us so we can demonstrate each technique.

> Bouncing is an easy repeating of the beginning of a word. While it may seem like stuttering, it is not, because it's relaxed, rhythmic, and forward flowing. It's a way of easing into a word and can be used on any sound.

> Sliding is an easy holding out of the first sound of a word. While it also may seem like stuttering, it is not, because it's relaxed and forward flowing. Like bouncing, it's a way of easing into a word. Unlike bouncing, it can only be used on sounds that continue (e.g., vowels and *s, z, f, v, m, n, h, y, r, l, sh,* and *th*).

> Light contacts and easy onsets are very similar. Light contacts are for consonants and easy onsets are for vowels. When you light contact a consonant, you bring your speech articulators (tongue, lips, teeth, roof of the mouth) together gently. You can light contact any consonant, but light contacts are especially helpful for *p, b, t, d, k, g, ch,* and *j*. Easy onsets are used for vowels. You bring your vocal folds together gently as you produce the vowel.

I'll teach your child each technique separately and then we'll combine them. Your child will be learning new habits of speech production. It takes a lot of practice to learn new habits so we'll practice the techniques in many structured activities. First, we'll produce them in unison and imitation. We'll then practice them in stereotyped (e.g., "I pick a card. I need it.") and carrier (e.g., "I found a _____. I need a _____.") sentences, questions and answers, and short sentences which we create. To add fun, some of the activities will be game-oriented. We can't expect your child to use these techniques in conversation yet.

I hope you find this information helpful. We look forward to demonstrating the techniques for you soon. If you have questions, please contact me. Your input and support are extremely helpful.

Sincerely,

_____
Speech-Language Pathologist

School Letter 3.2A

Dear _____,

I'm enjoying working with _____. The focus of our work will now be on learning to use easy speech. Sometimes getting a word started is hard so we're going to learn four ways to start a word in an easy, relaxed, forward flowing manner. I'll share with you activity sheets describing the rules for each technique and I'll invite you to join us so we can demonstrate each technique.

Bouncing is an easy repeating of the beginning of a word. While it may seem like stuttering, it is not, because it's relaxed, rhythmic, and forward flowing. It's a way of easing into a word and can be used on any sound.

Sliding is an easy holding out of the first sound of a word. While it, too, may seem like stuttering, it is not, because it's relaxed and forward flowing. Like bouncing, it's a way of easing into a word. Unlike bouncing, it can only be used on sounds that continue like vowels and *s, z, f, v, m, n, h, y, r, l, sh,* and *th*.

Light contacts and easy onsets are very similar. Light contacts are for consonants and easy onsets are for vowels. When you light contact a consonant, you bring your speech articulators (tongue, lips, teeth, roof of the mouth) together gently. You can light contact any consonant, but light contacts are especially helpful for *p, b, t, d, k, g, ch,* and *j*. Easy onsets are used for vowels. You bring your vocal folds together gently as you produce the vowel.

It takes a lot of practice to learn new speech production habits so we'll practice the techniques in many structured activities. First, we'll produce them in unison and imitation. We'll then practice them in stereotyped (e.g., "I pick a card. I need it.") and carrier (e.g., "I found a _____. I need a _____.") sentences, questions and answers, and short sentences which we create. To add fun, some of the activities will be game-oriented. We can't expect _____ to use these techniques in conversation yet.

I hope you find this information helpful. We look forward to demonstrating the techniques for you soon. If you have questions, please contact me. Your input and support are extremely helpful.

Sincerely,

_____
Speech-Language Pathologist

Home Letter 3.2B

Dear Family,

As you know, we've been working on using bouncing, sliding, light contacts, and easy onsets in speech class. These techniques for starting a word can be used in three ways: to cancel a stutter, to pull-out of a stutter, and to avoid a stutter by preparing ahead. Your child will be bringing home activity sheets that describe these cancellations, pull-outs, and preparatory sets, and we'll be inviting you to attend a session so we can demonstrate them for you.

A cancellation is when a person stutters and then immediately repeats the stuttered word using bouncing, sliding, a light contact, or an easy onset. In this way, the person cancels out the stuttering and replaces it with easy speech. The person has a sense of control and gains confidence. Cancelling is very hard because it interrupts the message, but it's an important step in taking charge of speech production.

A pull-out is when a person starts to stutter and then uses bouncing, sliding, a light contact, or an easy onset to pull-out of the stuttering before finishing the word. The person really catches the stuttering and changes it to easy speech in mid-stream.

A preparatory set is when a person decides ahead of time to use bouncing, sliding, a light contact, or an easy onset on a word. The person produces easy speech instead of stuttering.

Your child is making great progress toward our goal of easy speech. Working on cancellations, pull-outs, and preparatory sets is one more step in our climb. I'm excited about your child's progress. I hope you are, too. Be sure to let your child know how proud you are of the work being done.

If you have questions, please contact me. Your support and encouragement are invaluable.

Sincerely,

_____
Speech-Language Pathologist

School Letter 3.2B

Dear _____,

We've been working on using bouncing, sliding, light contacts, and easy onsets in speech class. These techniques for starting a word can be used in three ways: to cancel a stutter, to pull-out of a stutter, and to avoid a stutter by preparing ahead. I'll be sharing activity sheets that describe these cancellations, pull-outs, and preparatory sets, and we'll be inviting you to attend a session so we can demonstrate them for you.

A cancellation is when a person stutters and then immediately repeats the stuttered word using bouncing, sliding, a light contact, or an easy onset. In this way, the person cancels out the stuttering and replaces it with easy speech. The person has a sense of control and gains confidence. Cancelling is very hard because it interrupts the message, but it's an important step in taking charge of speech production.

A pull-out is when a person starts to stutter and then uses bouncing, sliding, a light contact, or an easy onset to pull-out of the stuttering before finishing the word. The person really catches the stuttering and changes it to easy speech in mid-stream.

A preparatory set is when a person decides ahead of time to use bouncing, sliding, a light contact, or an easy onset on a word. In this way, the person produces easy speech instead of stuttering.

We're making great progress toward our goal of easy speech. Working on cancellations, pull-outs, and preparatory sets is one more step in our climb. Please continue to provide support and encouragement — they're invaluable.

If you have questions, please contact me. I really appreciate your input.

Sincerely,

_____
Speech-Language Pathologist

Home Letter 4

Dear Family,

We're now beginning work on Step 4, using easy speech in the presence of disrupters. The goal is to continue to use easy speech by resisting conditions which might impact negatively on fluency. These disrupting conditions will be introduced gradually in structured tasks with which your child is already familiar.

Since the disrupters affecting fluency will vary from child to child, many disrupters will be used. People will be invited to join sessions, some by themselves and some in groups. Noise will be added to sessions like a tapping noise or a radio. Sometimes we'll complete our structured activities in new locations. At other times, I'll make errors and expect your child to correct me. I'll also be interrupting the activities and adding movement. For example, while completing activities, your child will be expected to throw a ball or draw a picture. I'll introduce another disrupter, time pressures, as I increase my rate of speech or tell your child to "hurry up." Competition will also be addressed by adding competitive comments and modeling good sportsmanship.

It won't be easy to continue using easy speech with these disrupters, but it's important for your child to learn to ignore disrupters. When dealing with the "outside world," your child will confront disrupters and we want to be sure that s/he is able to maintain use of easy speech when they occur.

Your continued input is important so I'll be contacting you shortly to be sure that we concentrate on situations which you feel might be particularly disruptive for your child. Meanwhile, continue to model easy speech as you talk with your child. It's important that you realize the complexity of the task your child is involved with right now. Your support is critical.

If you have questions, please feel free to call or send me a note. I'll get back to you as soon as possible.

Sincerely,

_____
Speech-Language Pathologist

School Letter 4

Dear _____,

_____ and I are now beginning work on Step 4, using easy speech in the presence of disrupters. The goal is to continue to use easy speech by resisting conditions which might impact negatively on fluency. These disrupting conditions will be introduced gradually in structured tasks with which your student is already familiar.

Since the disrupters affecting fluency will vary from child to child, many disrupters will be used. People will be invited to join sessions, some by themselves and some in groups. Noise will be added to sessions like a tapping noise or a radio. Sometimes we'll complete our structured activities in new locations. At other times, I'll make errors and expect your student to correct me. I'll also be interrupting the activities and adding movement. For example, while completing activities, your student will be expected to throw a ball or draw a picture. I'll introduce another disrupter, time pressures, as I increase my rate of speech or tell your student to "hurry up." Competition will also be addressed by adding competitive comments and modeling good sportsmanship.

It won't be easy to continue using easy speech with these disrupters, but it's important for your student to learn to ignore the disrupters. When dealing with the "outside world," your student will be confronted with disrupters and we want to be sure that s/he is able to maintain use of easy speech when they occur.

Your continued input is important so I'll be contacting you shortly to be sure that we concentrate on situations which you feel might be particularly disruptive for your student. Meanwhile, continue to model easy speech. It's important that you realize the complexity of the task your student is involved with right now. Your support is critical.

If you have questions, please feel free to call or send me a note. I'll get back to you as soon as possible.

Sincerely,

_____
Speech-Language Pathologist

Home Letter 5

Dear Family,

We've now reached the most exciting (and also most difficult) step in our climb to learning easy speech — Transfer of Easy Speech. We'll be working on transferring the speech production techniques we've been practicing in structured activities to real-life situations.

We'll be practicing easy speech in tasks that involve:

- informing (e.g., giving and getting information, making announcements, giving reports, explaining procedures)
- ritualizing (e.g., making introductions, using the phone, taking orders, ordering in a restaurant)
- controlling (e.g., giving warnings, asking for assistance, giving commands, negotiating)
- expressing feelings (e.g., apologizing, responding to teasing, discussing emotional topics, compromising)
- imagining (e.g., taking on another person's role)

We'll start by structuring the tasks and then move to semi-structured and spontaneous speaking situations. We'll do a lot of role-playing and then move to real-life activities at home, school, and in the community. As we progress through this step, your child will gain a sense of confidence and control regarding speech production.

You can help by attending some sessions and joining in our role-playing. You can also help your child complete any transfer assignments. If you know of difficult speaking situations, let me know so we can incorporate them into our sessions.

Your child deserves a lot of credit. Working on speech is hard work. Please offer words of encouragement and praise. I'm proud of the progress being made, as I'm sure you are, too.

If you have any questions, feel free to contact me.

Sincerely,

_____
Speech-Language Pathologist

School Letter 5

Dear _____,

We've now reached the most exciting (and also most difficult) step in our climb to learning easy speech — Transfer of Easy Speech. We'll be working on transferring the speech production techniques we've been practicing in structured activities to real-life situations.

We'll be practicing easy speech in tasks that involve:

- informing (e.g., giving and getting information, making announcements, giving reports, explaining procedures)
- ritualizing (e.g., making introductions, using the phone, taking orders, ordering in a restaurant)
- controlling (e.g., giving warnings, asking for assistance, giving commands, negotiating)
- expressing feelings (e.g., apologizing, responding to teasing, discussing emotional topics, compromising)
- imagining (e.g., taking on another person's role)

We'll start with structured tasks and then move to semi-structured and spontaneous speaking situations. We'll do a lot of role-playing and then move to real-life activities at home, school, and in the community. As we progress through this step, your student will gain a sense of confidence and control regarding speech production.

You can help by attending some sessions and joining in our role-playing. If you know of difficult classroom situations or upcoming speaking assignments, let me know so we can incorporate them into our sessions. You can also help by providing input for classroom transfer assignments.

Working on speech is hard work. Please offer words of encouragement and praise for the efforts being made. If you have any questions, feel free to contact me.

       Sincerely,

       _____
       Speech-Language Pathologist

Home Letter 6

Dear Family,

Your child has made excellent progress and it's now time to begin to reduce direct therapy contacts. If your child continues to be fluent, the time between direct contacts will be gradually increased. At first, continue to use easy speech at home and continue to complete the home activities routinely. Then, if your child maintains fluency, home activities can be gradually reduced. I'll be providing you with a schedule on how we'll accomplish this step.

Even though direct contact will be reduced, it's important to stay in touch. I'll ask you to call or drop me a note from time to time so I'll know how things are going at home. While I don't expect regression to occur, please call me if you have concerns. There are a number of things to do, but it's important to begin them right away. Meanwhile, remember to use easy speech — your continued model is important.

I've enjoyed working with you and your child. Your assistance has been much appreciated!

Sincerely,

_____
Speech-Language Pathologist

School Letter 6

Dear _____,

_____ has made excellent progress and it's now time to begin to reduce direct therapy contacts. If the student continues to be fluent, the time between direct contacts will be gradually increased. I'll be setting up a maintenance schedule with the family which will involve gradually reducing the number of therapy sessions as well as reducing home practice times.

Even though direct contact will be reduced, it's important to keep in contact. While I don't expect regression to occur, please let me know if you have concerns. There are a number of things to do, but it's important to begin them right away. Meanwhile, it will be helpful if you continue to use easy speech — your model is important.

I'm excited about the progress we've seen and I've appreciated your willingness to work with me. Thanks!

Sincerely,

_____
Speech-Language Pathologist

1-14-20

Copyright © 1998 LinguiSystems, Inc.

#31090A